petits fours

a fine selection of sweet treats

MURDOCH BOOKS

Contents

Delicate flowers

Bring a touch of exquisite beauty into your world with this tempting array of dainty morsels.

Mini cherry galettes

MAKES 30

670 g (1 lb 7½ oz) jar pitted morello cherries, drained
30 g (1 oz) unsalted butter
1½ tablespoons caster (superfine) sugar
1 egg yolk
½ teaspoon natural vanilla extract
55 g (2 oz/½ cup) ground almonds
1 tablespoon plain (all-purpose) flour
2 sheets ready-rolled puff pastry
icing (confectioners') sugar, sifted, for dusting
160 g (5¾ oz/½ cup) cherry jam, melted

Preheat the oven to 180°C (350°F/Gas 4). Line a baking tray with baking paper.

Spread the cherries on several sheets of paper towel to absorb any excess liquid.

Combine the butter and caster sugar in a medium bowl and beat until pale and fluffy. Add the egg yolk and vanilla, then stir in the combined ground almonds and flour. Refrigerate until required.

Cut 30 rounds from the pastry sheets using a 5 cm (2 inch) cutter. Place half the rounds on the prepared tray and lightly prick all over with a fork. Cover with another sheet of baking paper and weigh down with another baking tray—this prevents the pastry from rising during cooking. Bake for 10 minutes, remove from the oven and allow to cool on the tray. Repeat with the remaining rounds.

Spread ½ level teaspoon of the almond mixture over each cooled pastry round, then press three cherries onto the almond mixture. Bake for 10 minutes, or until lightly browned. Cool slightly and dust lightly with the icing sugar. Glaze the cherries by drizzling them with the warmed jam.

NOTE: The almond topping can be prepared up to 4 days in advance. Assemble the cherry galettes on the day they are to be eaten so that the pastry base doesn't go soggy.

Coffee and sugar crystal meringues

Preheat the oven to 120°C (235°F/Gas ½). Line two baking trays with baking paper.

Beat the egg whites in a bowl with electric beaters until stiff peaks form. Gradually add the caster sugar, beating continuously, until the sugar is dissolved and the mixture is thick and glossy.

Beat in the coffee powder until the mixture is slightly coloured. Sift the icing sugar and quickly fold into the mixture with the walnuts. Drop rounded teaspoons of the mixture well apart, to allow for spreading, onto the prepared trays.

Sprinkle with the coffee sugar crystals and bake for 25 minutes, or until crisp and dry. Turn off the oven and leave the meringues to cool completely in the oven with the door ajar.

NOTE: It is best to chop the walnuts by hand.

MAKES 40

2 egg whites
145 g (5¼ oz/⅔ cup) caster (superfine) sugar
1 teaspoon instant coffee powder
1 tablespoon icing (confectioners') sugar
40 g (1½ oz/⅓ cup) chopped walnuts
2 tablespoons coffee sugar crystals

Hazelnut brittle

MAKES 24

220 g (7¾ oz/1 cup) sugar
125 ml (4 fl oz/½ cup) water
35 g (1¼ oz/¼ cup) hazelnuts, lightly toasted,
skinned and roughly chopped
finely grated zest of 1 orange

Line a 30 x 25 cm (12 x 10 inch) baking tray with baking paper.

Combine the sugar and water in a small heavy-based saucepan over medium–high heat and stir well until the sugar has dissolved. Cook without stirring, brushing down the sides with a pastry brush if necessary, for 10–12 minutes, or until golden. Quickly add the hazelnuts and zest and stir to combine. Pour immediately onto the prepared baking tray, spreading to cover the whole surface. Allow to cool.

Break into bite-sized pieces. Store in an airtight container.

NOTE: Toast the hazelnuts in a 180°C (350°F/Gas 4) oven for 5–10 minutes, or until lightly golden. Tip the nuts onto a clean tea towel (dish towel) and rub gently to remove the skins.

Mini raspberry and frangipane tarts

Place the butter and flour in the bowl of a food processor and process until fine breadcrumbs form. Add the sugar and egg yolk and process until the dough just comes together, adding ½ tablespoon iced water if necessary. Turn out onto a lightly floured work surface and gather into a ball. Wrap in plastic wrap and refrigerate for 30 minutes.

Meanwhile, preheat the oven to 180°C (350°F/Gas 4). Lightly grease 24, 5 cm (2 inch) fluted mini tartlet tins or two 12-hole mini muffin tins.

Divide the pastry in half. Roll out each piece between two sheets of baking paper until 2 mm (¹⁄₁₆ inch) thick, scattering with flour where necessary. Cut 24 rounds from the pastry with a 6 cm (2½ inch) cutter. Line each prepared tin with a circle of pastry and trim off any excess. Prick the bases with a fork. Place in the freezer for 5 minutes. Line the bases with baking paper, pour in some baking beads or uncooked rice and bake for 5 minutes. Remove the paper and beads and bake for another 2–3 minutes, or until just golden. Set aside to cool.

To make the filling, beat the sugar and butter in a medium bowl using electric beaters for 30 seconds. Add the egg and vanilla and beat for another 30 seconds. Fold in the ground almonds, flour and chocolate. Spoon the filling into the cooled pastry cases. Press a raspberry into the top of each. Bake for 8–10 minutes, or until the filling is golden and set. Remove from the tins by turning upside down and tapping with the back of a knife handle. Dust with extra icing sugar, if desired.

MAKES 24

125 g (4½ oz/½ cup) unsalted butter, chilled and cut into cubes
155 g (5½ oz/1¼ cups) plain (all-purpose) flour
55 g (2 oz) icing (confectioners') sugar, plus extra, sifted, for dusting (optional)
1 large egg yolk
120 g (4¼ oz) raspberries

Filling
55 g (2 oz/¼ cup) sugar
60 g (2¼ oz/¼ cup) unsalted butter, softened
1 large egg
1 teaspoon natural vanilla extract
55 g (2 oz/½ cup) ground almonds
1 tablespoon plain (all-purpose) flour
60 g (2¼ oz) white chocolate, roughly chopped

Delicate flowers

Sesame and ginger wafers

Preheat the oven to 190°C (375°F/Gas 5). Grease two baking trays.

Combine the butter, sugar and syrup in a small saucepan and heat gently, stirring occasionally, until the butter melts and the mixture is smooth. Remove from the heat.

Sift the flour and ginger into a bowl. Add the melted butter mixture and the brandy, lemon juice and sesame seeds and stir to mix well.

Drop ½ teaspoon of the mixture onto the prepared trays (only cook four biscuits per tray), leaving enough room to allow for spreading. Use a spatula to spread each biscuit out to form a 5 cm (2 inch) round. Bake for 3–4 minutes, or until the wafers begin to brown around the edges. Cool for 1 minute. Using the palette knife and working quickly, carefully remove the warm biscuits from the trays, then drape them over the handle of a wooden spoon to make them curl. Cool completely, then remove from the wooden spoon. Repeat with the remaining mixture.

Sesame and ginger wafers are best eaten on the day they are made.

MAKES 36

40 g (1½ oz) unsalted butter
40 g (1½ oz) caster (superfine) sugar
2 tablespoons golden syrup (light treacle) or dark corn syrup
40 g (1½ oz/⅓ cup) plain (all-purpose) flour
½ teaspoon ground ginger
1 tablespoon brandy
2 teaspoons lemon juice
1 tablespoon sesame seeds, toasted

Lavender and honey madeleines

MAKES 30

30 g (1 oz) unsalted butter
2 teaspoons honey
2½ tablespoons caster (superfine) sugar
½ teaspoon dried lavender
30 g (1 oz/¼ cup) plain (all-purpose) flour
1½ tablespoons ground almonds
1 large egg, at room temperature
1 tablespoon icing (confectioners') sugar, sifted,
for dusting (optional)

Preheat the oven to 180°C (350°F/Gas 4). Use a pastry brush to lightly grease 30 mini madeleine moulds.

Melt the butter and honey in a small saucepan over medium heat. Set aside to cool. Place the caster sugar and lavender in the bowl of a food processor and process until combined. Sift the flour, ground almonds and a pinch of salt three times onto baking paper. (This will help to lighten the texture of the madeleines.)

Beat the egg and sugar mixture in a bowl with electric beaters until thick and creamy. Add the flour mixture and the cooled butter mixture and fold in lightly with a metal spoon until just combined. Allow to stand for 10 minutes. Spoon into the prepared madeleine moulds until three-quarters full. Bake for 6–8 minutes, or until lightly golden. Carefully remove from the moulds and place on a wire rack to cool. Dust lightly with icing sugar, if desired, before serving.

Madeleines should be served the same day they are baked.

Petits pithiviers

Lightly grease two baking trays.

To make the almond filling, cream the butter and sugar with electric beaters until pale and fluffy. Add the egg yolk and beat well. Stir in the ground almonds, orange zest and almond extract.

Lay the puff pastry on a work surface and cut into 48 rounds with a 5 cm (2 inch) cutter. Place about 1½ teaspoons of the almond filling on half the rounds, leaving a 5 mm (¼ inch) border. Brush the border with the beaten egg. Put the remaining pastry rounds over the filling and press the edges firmly to seal. Transfer to the prepared trays and refrigerate for 30 minutes.

Preheat the oven to 210°C (415°F/Gas 6–7).

With a blunt-edged knife, gently press up the pastry edges at intervals. Carefully score the pastry tops into wedges, then brush with the remaining beaten egg.

Bake for 10 minutes, or until lightly golden.

MAKES 24

3 sheets ready-rolled puff pastry
1 egg, lightly beaten

Almond filling
40 g (1½ oz) butter, softened
40 g (1½ oz/⅓ cup) icing (confectioners') sugar
1 egg yolk
70 g (2½oz/⅔ cup) ground almonds
1 teaspoon finely grated orange zest
few drops of natural almond extract

Mexican wedding cookies

MAKES 60

250 g (9 oz/1 cup) unsalted butter, softened
60 g (2¼ oz/½ cup) icing (confectioners') sugar
1 teaspoon natural almond extract
1 teaspoon natural vanilla extract
250 g (9 oz/2 cups) plain (all-purpose) flour, sifted
55 g (2 oz/½ cup) ground almonds
60 g (2¼ oz/½ cup) icing (confectioners') sugar, extra, sifted, for dusting

Cream the butter and sugar in a large bowl with electric beaters until pale and fluffy. Add the almond and vanilla extracts and beat until combined. Add the flour and ground almonds and use a metal spoon to mix to a soft dough. Gather the dough into a ball, then cover with plastic wrap. Refrigerate for 1–2 hours, or until firm.

Preheat the oven to 170°C (325°F/Gas 3). Line two large baking trays with baking paper.

Roll teaspoons of the cookie mixture into balls and place on the prepared trays. Bake for 12–15 minutes, or until lightly golden. Allow to cool on the trays for 5 minutes, then transfer to a wire rack to cool completely. While still warm, dust with the sifted icing sugar. Just before serving, dredge heavily with the sifted sugar again. When completely cool, store in an airtight container.

Chocolate-dipped strawberries

Line a baking tray with baking paper.

Melt the dark chocolate in a small heatproof bowl over a saucepan of simmering water, making sure the bowl does not touch the water. Dip the bottom half of each strawberry in the chocolate, transfer to the prepared baking tray and leave to set.

When set, melt the white chocolate in a small heatproof bowl over a saucepan of simmering water, making sure the base of the bowl does not touch the water, then dip the tips of the strawberries in the chocolate. Return to the baking tray and allow to set.

MAKES 12

12 large strawberries
150 g (5½ oz) good-quality dark chocolate, roughly chopped
100 g (3½ oz) good-quality white chocolate, roughly chopped

Buttered Brazil nuts

MAKES ABOUT 24

440 g (15½ oz/2 cups) sugar
2 tablespoons liquid glucose
125 g (4½ oz/½ cup) butter, chopped
1 tablespoon white vinegar
125 ml (4 fl oz/½ cup) water
310 g (11 oz/2 cups) whole Brazil nuts

Line two 33 x 28 cm (13 x 11¼ inch) baking trays with baking paper.

Combine the sugar, glucose, butter, vinegar and water in a medium heavy-based saucepan. Stir over medium heat without boiling, brushing the sugar crystals from the side of the pan with a wet pastry brush, until the butter has melted and the sugar has completely dissolved. Bring to the boil, then reduce the heat slightly and boil, without stirring, for 25 minutes, or until a teaspoon of the mixture dropped into cold water reaches soft-crack stage (forming little sticky threads) or, if using a sugar (candy) thermometer, it must reach 138°C (280°F). Remove from the heat immediately.

Working quickly, place one nut at a time on a wooden spoon and dip into the caramel mixture. Transfer to a prepared tray to set. Put sheets of baking paper between layers of the nuts and store in an airtight container at room temperature for up to 7 days.

NOTE: While Brazil nuts are traditionally used in this recipe, different types of nut or a combination can be used. Use the quantity given (by weight). If using smaller nuts, dip a few at a time to form clusters.

Shredded kataifi pastries

Preheat the oven to 170°C (325°F/Gas 3). Brush a 20 x 30 cm (8 x 12 inch) baking tray with some of the melted butter.

Place the ground nuts in a bowl with 55 g (2 oz/¼ cup) caster sugar, the ground cinnamon, ground cloves and brandy. Add the egg white and stir to make a paste. Divide the mixture into eight portions and roll each into a log about 18 cm (7 inches) long.

Take a handful of the pastry strands and spread them out on a work surface, with the strands running lengthways towards you, to measure 25 x 18 cm (10 x 7 inches). Brush with some of the melted butter. Cut the pastry in half. Place one of the nut logs at the end of the pastry nearest to you and roll up into a neat log shape. Repeat with the other pastry portions and nut logs. Place the pastry rolls close together on the prepared baking tray and brush with more melted butter. Bake for 50 minutes, or until golden brown.

Place the remaining sugar in a small saucepan with the water and stir over low heat until dissolved. Add the lemon juice, zest, whole cloves and cinnamon stick and boil for 10 minutes. Stir in the honey and set aside to cool.

When the pastries come out of the oven, pour the cold syrup over the top. Leave to cool completely before cutting each roll into five pieces.

MAKES 40

250 g (9 oz/1 cup) unsalted butter, melted
70 g (2½ oz/½ cup) ground pistachios
100 g (3½ oz/1 cup) ground almonds
510 g (1 lb 2¼ oz) caster (superfine) sugar
½ teaspoon ground cinnamon
pinch of ground cloves
2 teaspoons brandy
1 egg white, lightly beaten
500 g (1 lb 2 oz) kataifi pastry (Greek shredded pastry), left at room temperature for 2 hours (in its packaging)
500 ml (17 fl oz/2 cups) water
1 teaspoon lemon juice
5 cm (2 inch) strip lemon zest
4 whole cloves
1 cinnamon stick
1 tablespoon honey

Lemon curd and blueberry tartlets

MAKES 48

4 sheets ready-rolled shortcrust pastry
2 tablespoons icing (confectioners') sugar, sifted
48 blueberries

Lemon curd
150 ml (5 fl oz) lemon juice
2 teaspoons finely grated lemon zest
6 egg yolks
110 g (3¾ oz/½ cup) sugar
100 g (3½ oz) unsalted butter, cut into cubes

To make the lemon curd, whisk the lemon juice and zest, egg yolks and sugar in a small saucepan. Place over low heat and cook for 2–3 minutes, or until the sugar has dissolved. Gradually add the butter, stirring constantly, and cook for 8–10 minutes, or until thick. Remove from the heat and cover the surface with plastic wrap to prevent a skin forming. Refrigerate until needed.

Preheat the oven to 180°C (350°F/Gas 4). Lightly grease 24, 3 cm (1¼ inch) tartlet tins. Line a baking tray with baking paper.

Cut 48 rounds from the pastry with a 5 cm (2 inch) cutter. Place half the rounds on the prepared baking tray, cover with plastic wrap and refrigerate until needed. Press the remaining pastry rounds into the prepared tins. Bake the cases for 12–15 minutes, or until golden. Repeat with the remaining rounds. Allow to cool completely.

When cool, dust each tartlet case with the icing sugar, spoon in 1 teaspoon of the lemon curd and top with a blueberry.

These tartlets are best eaten the day they are made. The cases can be baked up to 1 week in advance and stored in an airtight container. To revive them, heat in a 180°C (350°F/Gas 4) oven for 5 minutes. The curd can be made 2 days ahead. Assemble no more than 1 hour before serving.

Coconut macaroons

Combine the egg whites, sugar and liquid glucose in a large heatproof bowl and whisk to combine. Place the bowl over a saucepan of simmering water and whisk until the mixture is just warm. Remove from the heat and add the vanilla, coconut and flour and stir to combine well. Cover the bowl with plastic wrap and refrigerate until firm.

Meanwhile, preheat the oven to 150°C (300°F/Gas 2). Line two baking trays with baking paper.

Take heaped teaspoons of the mixture and, with wet hands, form into balls. Flatten the balls slightly and place them on the prepared trays, spacing them well apart to allow for spreading. Bake for 15 minutes, or until the macaroons are light golden, swapping the position of the trays halfway through cooking. Cool for 5 minutes on the trays, then transfer to a wire rack to cool completely.

Macaroons will keep, stored in an airtight container, for up to 1 week, or frozen for up to 8 weeks.

MAKES 64

4 egg whites, lightly beaten
450 g (1 lb/2 cups) caster (superfine) sugar
1½ tablespoons liquid glucose
1½ teaspoons natural vanilla extract
175 g (6 oz/2 cups) desiccated coconut
125 g (4½ oz/1 cup) plain (all-purpose) flour

Mango and coconut napoleons

MAKES 12

1 sheet ready-rolled puff pastry
60 g (2¼ oz/¼ cup) unsalted butter, melted
40 g (1½ oz/⅓ cup) icing (confectioners') sugar,
plus extra, sifted, for dusting (optional)
1 ripe mango
125 ml (4 fl oz/½ cup) cream
1 teaspoon natural coconut extract

Preheat the oven to 200°C (400°F/Gas 6). Line two baking trays with baking paper.

Use a 4 cm (1½ inch) heart-shaped cookie cutter to cut 24 hearts from the pastry. Place 12 hearts on each prepared tray. Prick the hearts on one tray all over with a fork to form the bases. Place in the freezer for 2 minutes. Cover each tray with a sheet of baking paper and top with another tray to flatten the pastry hearts. Bake for 4–5 minutes. Remove the top tray from the hearts that will form the lids and brush with the melted butter — this will allow them to rise. Bake the other tray for a further 2 minutes before removing the top tray and brushing the hearts with butter. Return both trays to the oven and cook for a further 1–2 minutes, or until crisp and golden. Transfer onto a wire rack to cool completely.

Preheat the grill (broiler) to medium–high. Dredge the hearts with 2 tablespoons of the icing sugar. Place on the unlined baking trays and place under the grill for 1–2 minutes, or until light golden and caramelised. Slice the mango into 2–3 mm (¹⁄₁₆–⅛ inch) thick slices. Cut out 24 heart shapes using the cookie cutter.

Whisk the cream, the remaining icing sugar and the coconut extract until firm peaks form. Place a mango heart on each pastry base and spread on a thin layer of cream. Add another mango heart and a layer of cream and top with the lids. Dust with extra icing sugar, if desired, and serve immediately. The napoleons are best eaten the day they are made.

Brandy snap flowers

Preheat the oven to 180°C (350°F/Gas 4). Lightly grease two baking trays.

Place the butter, sugar, golden syrup, chicory essence, coffee and brandy in a small saucepan. Stir over low heat until the butter melts and the sugar dissolves. Remove from the heat and stir in the flour and ginger.

Drop ¼ teaspoons of the mixture well apart onto the prepared trays (only cook a maximum of four biscuits per tray). Bake for 3–4 minutes, or until golden. Be careful not to allow the brandy snaps to burn. Leave for 1–2 minutes, then press into the base of muffin mini tins to curl the brandy snaps. Set aside.

If using the melted chocolate, drizzle the chocolate over the base of the biscuits and allow to set.

Brandy snaps will keep, stored in an airtight container, for 2–3 days.

MAKES 88

50 g (1¾ oz) unsalted butter

55 g (2 oz/¼ cup) soft brown sugar

1 tablespoon golden syrup (light treacle)

1 teaspoon chicory essence (camp coffee)

½ teaspoon instant coffee powder

2 teaspoons brandy

40 g (1½ oz/⅓ cup) plain (all-purpose) flour

1 teaspoon ground ginger

200 g (7 oz) dark chocolate, melted (optional)

Greek shortbread crescents

MAKES 60

250 g (9 oz/1 cup) unsalted butter, softened
60 g (2¼ oz/½ cup) icing (confectioners') sugar
1 teaspoon finely grated orange zest
1 egg yolk
1 tablespoon brandy
55 g (2 oz/½ cup) ground almonds
40 g (1½ oz/¼ cup) blanched almonds, toasted and chopped
310 g (11 oz/2½ cups) plain (all-purpose) flour, sifted
1½ teaspoons baking powder, sifted
60 g (2¼ oz/½ cup) icing (confectioners') sugar, extra, sifted, for dusting

Cream the butter, sugar and orange zest in a small bowl with electric beaters until pale and fluffy. Add the egg yolk and brandy and beat until thoroughly combined. Transfer the mixture to a large bowl. Use a metal spoon to fold in the ground and blanched almonds, the flour and baking powder, and mix until well combined. Gather together and wrap in plastic wrap. Refrigerate for 1–2 hours, or until chilled.

Preheat the oven to 160°C (315°F/Gas 2–3). Line two large baking trays with baking paper.

Shape ½ tablespoons of the mixture into crescents, using lightly floured hands. Place on the prepared baking trays. Bake for 12–15 minutes, or until pale golden. Cool on the trays for 5 minutes, then transfer to a wire rack to cool completely. While still warm, dust with the sifted icing sugar. Just before serving, dredge heavily again with the icing sugar. When completely cool, store in an airtight container.

Cinnamon palmiers

Preheat the oven to 200°C (400°F/Gas 6). Line a large baking tray with baking paper.

Combine the sugar and cinnamon in a small bowl. Sprinkle half of the cinnamon sugar onto a clean work surface, place the pastry on top and sprinkle with the remaining cinnamon sugar. Gently roll over the pastry with a rolling pin to secure the sugar, brush with half the melted butter and slice in half. Use your fingers to gently roll up one long side as tightly as possible to the middle. Repeat with the remaining side and the remaining piece of pastry. Brush with the remaining butter. Wrap the rolls tightly in plastic wrap and freeze for 15–20 minutes, or until firm.

Use a small, sharp knife to cut across each roll into 1 cm (½ inch) thick slices. Place the palmiers, cut side up, 1–2 cm (½–¾ inch) apart, to allow for spreading, on the prepared tray. Bake for 8–10 minutes, or until beginning to caramelise. Remove the tray from the oven and carefully flip the palmiers. Bake for a further 2–3 minutes. Transfer to a wire rack to cool, caramelised side up.

Store in an airtight container for up to 1 week.

MAKES 50

55 g (2 oz/¼ cup) sugar
1 teaspoon ground cinnamon
1 x 25 cm (10 inch) square sheet ready-rolled
    puff pastry
30 g (1 oz) unsalted butter, melted

Orchard fruit candies

MAKES 80

200 g (7 oz) dried apricots
200 g (7 oz) dried pears, roughly chopped
400 g (14 oz) sugar
100 g (3½ oz) flaked almonds, toasted

Place the apricots and pears in separate saucepans and generously cover with water. Bring to the boil over low–medium heat and simmer for 40 minutes, or until tender. Check the water levels from time to time and add hot water if necessary to prevent the fruit from sticking to the saucepans.

When the fruit is tender, increase the heat and quickly boil off any excess water (otherwise the texture of the candies will be jammy rather than firm). Remove from the heat, add half the sugar to each pan and stir until the sugar dissolves. Place over low heat and bring to the boil. Simmer, stirring often, for 25–30 minutes, or until the mixture comes away from the side of the pan, but the texture is still a little chunky.

Line two 7 x 21 cm (2¾ x 8¼ inch) loaf (bar) tins with baking paper, extending the paper over the long sides for easy removal later. Pour the apricots into one tin and the pears into the other. Leave overnight to firm up.

Place the almonds in a shallow bowl and break them up a little with your hands. Use a knife dipped in cold water to cut the fruit slabs into 1 cm (½ inch) slices, then cut each slice in half. Toss the fruit bars in the almonds.

The fruit candies will keep, stored in an airtight container, for many weeks.

Amaretti

Line two baking trays with baking paper.

Sift the flours, cinnamon and half the caster sugar into a large bowl. Add the lemon zest and ground almonds.

Place the egg whites in a clean bowl and beat with electric beaters until soft peaks form. Gradually add the remaining caster sugar to the egg whites, beating constantly until the mixture is thick and glossy and all the sugar is dissolved. Fold into the dry ingredients with a metal spoon, until the mixture is just combined and forms a soft dough. With oiled or wet hands, roll 1 level teaspoon of the mixture at a time into a ball. Arrange the balls on the prepared baking trays, allowing room for spreading. Set aside, uncovered, for 1 hour.

Preheat the oven to 180°C (350°F/Gas 4).

Sift the icing sugar liberally over the biscuits. Bake for 10–12 minutes, or until crisp and lightly browned. Transfer to a wire rack to cool. Serve dusted with the extra icing sugar.

MAKES 48

1 tablespoon plain (all-purpose) flour
1 tablespoon cornflour (cornstarch)
1 teaspoon ground cinnamon
145 g (5¼ oz/⅔ cup) caster (superfine) sugar
1 teaspoon finely grated lemon zest
100 g (3½ oz/1 cup) ground almonds
2 egg whites
30 g (1 oz/¼ cup) icing (confectioners') sugar, plus extra, sifted, for dusting

Honeycomb

MAKES ABOUT 24 PIECES

325 g (11½ oz) caster (superfine) sugar
2 tablespoons honey
80 ml (2½ fl oz/⅓ cup) liquid glucose
80 ml (2½ fl oz/⅓ cup) water
1 tablespoon bicarbonate of soda (baking soda)
100 g (3½ oz/⅔ cup) chopped dark chocolate
(optional)

Grease a 20 x 30 cm (8 x 12 inch) baking tin and line with baking paper. Have ready a large metal bowl or saucepan, as the toffee will expand to triple in size when the bicarbonate of soda is added.

Place the sugar, honey, liquid glucose and water in a saucepan and stir over low heat until the sugar dissolves. Increase the heat to medium–high and boil the mixture without stirring, using a pastry brush dipped in cold water to brush down the side of the saucepan to remove any sugar crystals, until it reaches the hard-ball stage on a sugar (candy) thermometer (130°C/250°F) and turns light caramel in colour; this will take 7–8 minutes. Now working quickly, as you need to retain the heat for the bicarbonate of soda to aerate the toffee, pour the toffee into the large metal bowl, then immediately whisk in the bicarbonate of soda. The mixture will very quickly rise and will continue to colour with the heat. Pour it straight into the prepared tin. The mixture will continue to grow and expand at this stage. Roughly spread it out as best you can without disturbing the honeycomb too much, as this will disrupt the bubbling. Leave to cool for 20–30 minutes, or until set.

Cut the honeycomb into shards or rough squares. Place the chocolate in a heatproof bowl over a saucepan of gently simmering water, ensuring that the bowl doesn't touch the water. Stir frequently, until just melted and smooth. Dip the honeycomb pieces into the chocolate, or spread them out and drizzle the chocolate over the pieces at random. Store in an airtight container.

Rich and sophisticated

The elegance of yesteryear returns with these timeless classics.

Mini profiteroles

MAKES 48

60 g (2¼ oz/¼ cup) unsalted butter, chopped
250 ml (9 fl oz/1 cup) water
125 g (4½ oz/1 cup) plain (all-purpose)
flour, sifted
4 eggs, beaten
300 ml (10½ fl oz) cream
1 tablespoon icing (confectioners') sugar, sifted
½ teaspoon natural vanilla extract
50 g (1¾ oz) dark chocolate, melted

Preheat the oven to 200°C (400°F/Gas 6) and line two baking trays with baking paper.

Place the butter and water in a saucepan and stir over low heat until the butter melts. Bring to the boil, remove from the heat and add all the flour. Beat with a wooden spoon until smooth. Return to the heat and beat for 2 minutes, or until the mixture forms a ball and leaves the side of the pan. Remove from the heat and transfer to a bowl. Cool for 5 minutes. Add the egg, a little at a time, beating well after each addition, and continue beating until thick and glossy—a wooden spoon should stand upright in the mixture.

Spoon the mixture into a piping (icing) bag with a 1 cm (½ inch) fluted nozzle. Pipe 3 cm (1¼ inch) rounds of batter onto the prepared trays. Bake for 10 minutes, then reduce the heat to 180°C (350°F/Gas 4) and cook for a further 10 minutes, or until golden and puffed. Poke a hole in one side of each profiterole and remove the soft dough from inside with a teaspoon. Return the profiteroles to the oven for 2–3 minutes. Cool on a wire rack.

Whip the cream, sugar and vanilla until thick. Pipe the cream into the side of each profiterole. Dip each profiterole in the melted chocolate, face side down, then return to the wire rack for the chocolate to set.

Cherry almond nougat

Grease a 28 x 18 cm (11¼ x 7 inch) baking tin and line with baking paper, extending the paper over the long sides for easy removal later.

Place the sugar, liquid glucose, honey, water and ¼ teaspoon of salt in a heavy-based saucepan and stir over low heat until the sugar dissolves. Boil without stirring for 8 minutes, or until the mixture reaches hard-ball stage (forms a hard blob) or 121°C (250°F) on a sugar (candy) thermometer.

Beat the egg whites in a bowl using electric beaters until firm peaks form. Slowly pour a quarter of the syrup onto the egg whites in a thin stream and beat for up to 5 minutes, or until the mixture holds its shape. Place the remaining syrup over low heat and cook for 2 minutes, or until it reaches soft-crack stage (forming little sticky threads), or 143°C (290°F) on the thermometer. Pour slowly onto the meringue mixture with the beaters running and beat until very thick.

Add the vanilla and butter and beat for 5 minutes. Stir in the almonds and cherries using a metal spoon. Turn the mixture into the prepared tin and smooth the top with a spatula. Refrigerate for at least 4 hours, or until firm. Cut into pieces with a very sharp knife. Wrap each piece in cellophane and store in the refrigerator.

MAKES 60

440 g (15½ oz/2 cups) sugar
250 ml (9 fl oz/1 cup) liquid glucose
175 g (6 oz/½ cup) honey (preferably blossom honey)
60 ml (2 fl oz/¼ cup) water
2 egg whites
1 teaspoon natural vanilla extract
125 g (4½ oz/½ cup) unsalted butter, softened
50 g (1¾ oz/⅓ cup) almonds, toasted
105 g (3½ oz/½ cup) glacé (candied) cherries (not imitation)

Rich and sophisticated

Pecan and white chocolate biscotti

MAKES 90

155 g (5½ oz/1¼ cups) plain (all-purpose) flour
½ teaspoon baking powder
80 g (2¾ oz/⅓ cup) caster (superfine) sugar
2 eggs
½ teaspoon finely grated lemon zest
½ teaspoon natural vanilla extract
30 g (1 oz/¼ cup) lightly toasted chopped pecans
30 g (1 oz) white chocolate chips
100 g (3½ oz) white chocolate, roughly chopped

Preheat the oven to 170°C (325°F/Gas 3). Line two large baking trays with baking paper.

Sift the flour and baking powder into a bowl. Add the sugar and mix well. Make a well in the centre and add the eggs, lemon zest and vanilla. Use a large metal spoon to stir until just combined. Mix in the pecans and the chocolate chips. Knead for 2–3 minutes on a lightly floured surface. Divide the dough into two equal portions and, using lightly floured hands, roll each into a log about 25 cm (10 inches) long and 3 cm (1¼ inches) wide.

Place the logs on the prepared trays. Bake for 20–25 minutes, or until just golden and firm to the touch. Remove from the oven and cool slightly. Reduce the oven temperature to 150°C (300°F/Gas 2).

Cut each log into 5 mm (¼ inch) slices. Spread the biscotti well apart on the trays and bake for 6 minutes. Flip them over and cook for another 6 minutes, or until lightly golden and crisp. Transfer to a wire rack to cool completely.

Place the chopped chocolate in a heatproof bowl over a saucepan of simmering water, ensuring the bowl doesn't touch the water. Dip the biscotti in the chocolate or drizzle the chocolate over the biscotti with a spoon. Allow the chocolate to set. These biscotti will keep, stored in an airtight container, for up to 3 weeks.

Mini lime meringue pies

Preheat the oven to 180°C (350°F/Gas 4). Grease two 12-hole mini muffin tins.

Use a 7 cm (2¾ inch) cutter to cut 24 rounds from the pastry sheets. Press the rounds into the prepared tins and prick the bases well with a fork. Bake for 12–15 minutes, or until golden brown. Set aside to cool.

Combine the sugar, cornflour, lime zest and juice, and water in a large saucepan and stir over medium heat until the mixture boils and thickens. Remove from the heat and add the butter. Mix well and gradually stir in the egg yolks. Spoon 1 heaped teaspoon of the lime curd into each pastry case.

To make the meringue, beat the egg whites in a large bowl with electric beaters until stiff peaks form. Gradually add the sugar and beat until the sugar dissolves and the mixture is thick and glossy. Spoon or pipe 1 tablespoon of meringue over each pie. Bake for 4–5 minutes, or until lightly golden on top.

These pies will keep stored in an airtight container, for up to 2 days.

MAKES 24

4 sheets ready-rolled sweet shortcrust pastry
115 g (4 oz/½ cup) caster (superfine) sugar
30 g (1 oz/¼ cup) cornflour (cornstarch)
2 teaspoons finely grated lime zest
80 ml (2½ fl oz/⅓ cup) lime juice
185 ml (6 fl oz/¾ cup) water
30 g (1 oz) unsalted butter
2 egg yolks

Meringue
3 egg whites
170 g (6 oz/¾ cup) caster (superfine) sugar

Chocolate orange truffles

MAKES 40

185 ml (6 fl oz/¾ cup) thick
(double/heavy) cream
400 g (14 oz) good-quality dark
chocolate, grated
70 g (2½ oz) unsalted butter, chopped
2 tablespoons Cointreau
unsweetened cocoa powder, sifted, for coating

Place the cream in a small saucepan and bring to the boil. Remove from the heat, add the chocolate and stir until the chocolate has melted. Add the butter and stir until melted and smooth. Then stir in the Cointreau. Transfer to a bowl, cover and refrigerate overnight or until the mixture is firm enough to roll.

Quickly roll teaspoons of the mixture into balls, and refrigerate until firm. Roll the balls in the cocoa, shake off any excess and return to the refrigerator. Serve the truffles at room temperature.

Raspberry and coconut ice petits fours

MAKES 12

150 g (5½ oz) white chocolate, chopped

Coconut ice
105 g (1¼ oz/1 cup) icing (confectioners') sugar
80 ml (2½ fl oz/⅓ cup) sweetened
   condensed milk
45g (1⅔ oz/½ cup) desiccated coconut
20 g (¾ oz) Copha (white vegetable
   shortening), melted
1 small egg white

Sugar-coated raspberries
1 small egg white
125 g (4½ oz/1 cup) raspberries
55 g (2 oz/¼ cup) caster (superfine) sugar

Place the chocolate in a heatproof bowl over a saucepan of simmering water, ensuring that the bowl doesn't touch the water. Stir until the chocolate is melted. Paint the inside of 12 small paper cases evenly with half the chocolate. Place on a baking tray and transfer to the freezer until set. Paint again carefully with another layer of chocolate. Return to the freezer until set. Carefully peel off the paper cases.

To make the coconut ice, sift the sugar into a bowl. Add the condensed milk, coconut and Copha and stir until well combined. In a separate, clean bowl, beat the egg white until soft peaks form. Fold into the coconut mixture. Spoon the coconut ice into the chocolate cases and press flat with a teaspoon dipped in boiling water. Refrigerate until needed.

To make the sugar-coated raspberries, lightly whisk the egg white. Place a raspberry on a skewer, dip into the egg white and sprinkle with the sugar. Repeat with the remaining raspberries. Transfer to a plate covered with paper towel and allow to set.

Top each petit four with a sugar-coated raspberry and refrigerate until needed. These petits fours freeze well.

Mini mocha lamingtons

MAKES 48

125 g (4½ oz/½ cup) unsalted butter, chopped, softened
230 g (8¼ oz/1 cup) caster (superfine) sugar
½ teaspoon natural vanilla extract
2 eggs
250 g (9 oz/2 cups) self-raising flour
250 ml (9 fl oz/1 cup) milk
2 teaspoons instant coffee powder, dissolved in 2 teaspoons boiling water

Icing
375 g (13 oz/3 cups) icing (confectioners') sugar
60 g (2¼ oz/½ cup) unsweetened cocoa powder
20 g (¾ oz) unsalted butter, softened
2 teaspoons instant coffee powder
150 ml (5 fl oz) boiling water
75 g (2½ oz/1¼ cups) shredded coconut
90 g (3¼ oz/1 cup) desiccated coconut

Preheat the oven to 180°C (350°F/Gas 4). Lightly grease the base and sides of a 23 cm (9 inch) square baking tin and line the base with baking paper, extending the paper over two opposite sides for easy removal later.

Cream the butter, sugar and vanilla in a bowl using electric beaters until pale and fluffy. Add the eggs, one at a time, beating well after each addition. Sift the flour into a bowl, then stir the flour into the butter mixture alternately with the milk until combined and smooth. Spoon half the mixture into the prepared tin and spread evenly over the base. Add the coffee to the remaining mixture and stir until well combined. Carefully spread the coffee mixture over the mixture in the tin. Bake for 30–35 minutes, or until a skewer inserted in the centre of the cake comes out clean. Cool in the tin for 5 minutes before turning out onto a wire rack to cool completely. Cut into squares.

To make the icing, sift the sugar and cocoa into a large shallow bowl. Add the butter and coffee and gradually whisk in the water until smooth. Place the shredded and desiccated coconut in a large shallow bowl and toss to combine.

Using two spoons to hold the cake squares, dip each square in the icing to cover, allowing the excess to drip off. (Add a little boiling water to the icing if it starts to thicken.) Roll each square in the coconut to cover. Repeat with remaining squares.

Turkish delight squares

Brush an 18 x 10 cm (7 x 4 inch) baking tin with water.

Place the water in a heavy-based saucepan and sprinkle in the gelatine. Heat over low heat and stir until the gelatine dissolves. Add the sugar, zest and juice and continue stirring until the sugar dissolves. Bring to the boil and continue to boil for 8 minutes, stirring constantly. Discard the zest.

Stir the tartaric acid and rosewater into the mixture. Add the food colouring, 2–3 drops at a time, until a very pale pink is reached. Pour into the prepared tin and leave overnight to set (do not put in the refrigerator).

Sift the icing sugar and cornflour into a shallow bowl. Dust 3–4 tablespoons of the icing sugar mixture onto a cold hard surface (marble is ideal). Ease the Turkish delight away from the sides of the tin with your fingers and, starting at one end, peel it out of the tin. It tends to be sticky and will stretch a little, but it is quite resilient. Place the slab on the icing sugar-covered work surface.

Use an oiled knife to cut the Turkish delight into 2.5 cm (1 inch) squares. Toss them in the bowl of icing sugar mixture to coat all sides. Work with a few squares at a time to prevent the uncoated pieces from sticking together. Store in an airtight container, with baking paper between each layer. Turkish delight will keep for many weeks.

MAKES 28

280 ml (9¾ fl oz) cold water
3 tablespoons powdered gelatine
440 g (15½ oz/2 cups) sugar
1 strip lemon zest, no pith
½ teaspoon lemon juice
½ teaspoon tartaric acid
1–1½ teaspoons rosewater, or to taste
pink food colouring or cochineal
100 g (3½ oz) icing (confectioners') sugar
60 g (2¼ oz/½ cup) cornflour (cornstarch)

Rich and sophisticated

Baby choc chip scones

MAKES 81

250 g (9 oz/2 cups) self-raising flour
1 teaspoon baking powder
30 g (1 oz) unsalted butter, chilled and cut
into cubes
1 tablespoon caster (superfine) sugar
130 g (4¾ oz/¾ cup) milk chocolate chips
250 ml (9 fl oz/1 cup) milk
1 medium banana
icing (confectioners') sugar, sifted,
for dusting (optional)

Custard cream
125 ml (4 fl oz/½ cup) milk
30 g (1 oz) caster (superfine) sugar
1 egg yolk
½ teaspoon natural vanilla extract
1 tablespoon cornflour (cornstarch)
125 ml (4 fl oz/½ cup) cream

Preheat the oven to 200°C (400°F/Gas 6). Line a baking tray with baking paper. Sift the flour and baking powder into a bowl. Rub in the butter using your fingertips, then stir in the sugar and chocolate. Add the milk, reserving 2 tablespoons, and mix with a flat-bladed knife until the dough comes together. Tip onto a lightly floured surface and pat into a smooth ball — do not knead.

Gently pat the dough out until 2 cm (¾ inch) thick and 18 x 18 cm (7 x 7 inches) in size. Cut into 2 cm (¾ inch) squares. Place on the prepared baking tray and brush the tops with the reserved milk. Bake for 12–15 minutes, or until golden brown.

To make the custard cream, bring the milk and half the sugar to a simmer in a saucepan over medium heat. Whisk the egg yolk, remaining sugar, vanilla and cornflour in a bowl. Gradually pour in the hot milk mixture, whisking constantly. Pour the mixture into a clean saucepan and cook over medium–high heat, whisking constantly until thick. Allow to cool for 10 minutes. Transfer to a bowl. Cover and refrigerate until chilled. Meanwhile, whip the cream in a bowl until firm peaks form. Beat the custard with electric beaters until glossy. Gently fold in the cream until smooth.

To assemble, slice the scones in half. Thinly slice the banana and arrange two slices on top of each base. Top with a spoonful of custard cream. Finish with the lids. Dust with icing sugar, if desired, and serve immediately.

Marshmallow cherry blondies

Preheat the oven to 180°C (350°F/Gas 4). Lightly grease a 23 cm (9 inch) square cake tin and line the base and sides with baking paper, extending the paper over two opposite sides for easy removal later.

Place the butter and chocolate in a heatproof bowl. Half-fill a saucepan with water and bring to the boil. Place the bowl over the saucepan, ensuring the bowl does not touch the water. Stir occasionally until the butter and chocolate are melted and smooth. Transfer to a large bowl.

Add the caster sugar to the bowl and whisk in the eggs, one at a time. Add the vanilla, orange zest and cherries. Sift in the flour and baking powder and fold in until just combined. Pour into the prepared tin. Bake for 30–35 minutes, or until a skewer inserted into the centre comes out clean. If the top starts to brown too quickly, cover lightly with a sheet of foil. When cooked, cool in the tin before lifting out, using the paper as handles.

Use a 3 cm (1¼ inch) cutter to cut the blondies into rounds. Preheat the grill (broiler) to medium–high. Place half a marshmallow on each round. Grill for 1–2 minutes, or until golden and melted.

MAKES 30

125 g (4½ oz/½ cup) unsalted butter
200 g (7 oz) white chocolate, chopped
115 g (4 oz/½ cup) caster (superfine) sugar
3 eggs
1 teaspoon natural vanilla extract
2 teaspoons finely grated orange zest
210 g (7½ oz/1 cup) red glacé (candied) cherries, chopped
155 g (5½ oz/1¼ cups) plain (all-purpose) flour
1 teaspoon baking powder
120 g (4¼ oz/1⅓ cups) marshmallows, halved horizontally

Rich and sophisticated

Rocky road

MAKES 40

250 g (9 oz/2¾ cups) pink and white
marshmallows, halved
160 g (5¾ oz/1 cup) unsalted peanuts,
roughly chopped
105 g (3½ oz/½ cup) glacé (candied)
cherries, halved
60 g (2¼ oz/1 cup) shredded coconut
350 g (12 oz/2⅓ cups) chopped dark chocolate

Line the base and two opposite sides of a 20 cm
(8 inch) square baking tin with baking paper.

Place the marshmallows, peanuts, cherries and
coconut in a large bowl and mix until well combined.

Place the chocolate in a heatproof bowl over a
saucepan of simmering water, ensuring the bowl
doesn't touch the water. Stir occasionally until the
chocolate is just melted and smooth. Add the chocolate
to the marshmallow mixture and toss until well
combined. Spoon into the prepared tin and press
evenly over the base. Refrigerate for several hours, or
until set. Carefully lift out of the tin, peel away the
paper and cut the rocky road into small pieces.

Store the rocky road in an airtight container in the
refrigerator for up to 1 week.

Mini rum babas

To make the sauce, combine all the ingredients in a small saucepan over medium–high heat, stirring to dissolve the sugar. Bring to the boil, reduce heat to medium and simmer, without stirring, brushing the sugar from the side of the pan with a wet pastry brush as necessary, for 8 minutes, or until golden and syrupy. Remove the zest and slice very finely.

Preheat the oven to 170°C (325°F/Gas 3). Lightly spray 36 mini baba tins with oil.

Beat the egg white and a pinch of salt in a clean bowl until soft peaks form. Gradually add the sugar, and beat until thick and glossy and the sugar has dissolved. Add the egg yolk and vanilla and beat again.

Sift the flour onto baking paper three times. Heat the butter and milk in a small saucepan over medium heat until the butter has melted. Gently fold the flour and butter mixture into the egg mixture. Spoon into the prepared tins. Place on a baking tray and bake for 6–8 minutes, or until just starting to colour. Do not overcook. Carefully remove from the tins, while still warm and place on a serving plate.

Spoon over the warm sauce until the babas are well soaked. Spoon or pipe the cream onto the top of each baba. Garnish with slivers of orange zest. Serve warm or cold.

MAKES 36

1 egg, separated
55 g (2 oz/¼ cup) caster (superfine) sugar
¼ teaspoon natural vanilla extract
60 g (2¼ oz/½ cup) self-raising flour
30 g (1 oz) unsalted butter
30 ml (1 fl oz) milk
whipped cream, to serve

Sauce
170 g (6 oz/¾ cup) caster (superfine) sugar
185 ml (6 fl oz/¾ cup) rum
80 ml (2½ fl oz/⅓ cup) fresh orange juice, strained
80 ml (2½ fl oz/⅓ cup) fresh lime juice, strained
3 x 5 cm (2 inch) pieces orange zest

Ginger panforte

MAKES 30

40 g (1½ oz/⅓ cup) plain (all-purpose) flour
1 tablespoon unsweetened cocoa powder
1 teaspoon ground ginger
½ teaspoon ground cardamom
1 teaspoon ground cinnamon
125 g (4½ oz/⅔ cup) chopped dried figs
50 g (1¾ oz) glacé (candied) ginger, chopped
50 g (1¾ oz) glacé (candied) pineapple, chopped
50 g (1¾ oz) glacé (candied) apricots, chopped
50 g (1¾ oz) chopped mixed peel (mixed candied citrus peel)
175 g (6 oz) blanched almonds, toasted
80 g (2¾ oz/⅓ cup) caster (superfine) sugar
90 g (3¼ oz/¼ cup) honey
2 teaspoons water

Preheat the oven to 160°C (315°F/Gas 2–3). Lightly grease a 7 x 25 cm (2¾ x 10 inch) baking tin and line with baking paper, extending the paper over the two long sides for easy removal later.

Sift the flour, cocoa, ground ginger and spices into a large bowl. Add the fruit and almonds.

Heat the sugar, honey and water in a small saucepan over low heat, stirring until the sugar melts and the mixture just comes to the boil. Pour onto the dry ingredients and mix well. Press the mixture into the prepared tin and bake for 35–40 minutes, or until just firm. Cool in the tin, then chill until firm. Cut into thin pieces.

White chocolate bark

Preheat the oven to 180°C (350°F/Gas 4) and line a baking tray with baking paper.

Spread the nuts over a second baking tray and toast for 5–6 minutes, or until lightly browned, shaking the tray once or twice to ensure even toasting. Cool.

Place the chocolate in a heatproof bowl over a saucepan of simmering water, ensuring the bowl doesn't touch the water. Stir until the chocolate is just melted and smooth. Remove from the heat. Add two-thirds of the nuts and dried fruit and stir to coat.

Pour the mixture onto the prepared tray and spread to form a square of approximately 25 cm (10 inches). Scatter over the remaining nuts and dried fruit. Cover with plastic wrap and refrigerate until set.

Break into small chunks and store, in an airtight container, in the refrigerator for 3 weeks.

MAKES 8–10

160 g (5¾ oz/1 cup) unsalted macadamia
  nuts, chopped
225 g (8 oz/1⅔ cups) chopped white chocolate
120 g (4¼ oz/⅔ cup) dried apricots,
  finely chopped
50 g (1¾ oz/⅓ cup) currants

Chewy caramel walnut bites

MAKES 48

125 g (4½ oz/½ cup) unsalted butter,
cut into cubes
400 g (14 oz) tin sweetened condensed milk
2 tablespoons golden syrup (light treacle)
165 g (5¾ oz/¾ cup) soft brown sugar
100 g (3½ oz/1 cup) walnut halves, toasted,
finely chopped, plus extra, to decorate
400 g (14 oz/2⅔ cups) chopped dark chocolate

Grease an 18 cm (7 inch) square baking tin and line with baking paper, extending the paper over two opposite sides for easy removal later. Line a baking tray with baking paper.

Combine the butter, condensed milk, golden syrup and sugar in a saucepan and stir over low heat until the butter melts and the sugar dissolves. Increase the heat a little so that the mixture bubbles at a steady slow boil. Stir constantly for 9–10 minutes, or until caramel in colour and the mixture leaves the side of the pan when stirred. Stir in the walnuts. Pour into the prepared tin and leave at room temperature to set.

Remove from the tin, using the paper as handles. Cut into six even pieces. Gently roll each piece into a log approximately 18 cm (7 inches) long and place on the prepared tray. Refrigerate for 1 hour, or until firm. Cut each log into 2 cm (¾ inch) pieces.

Meanwhile, melt the chocolate in a heatproof bowl over a saucepan of simmering water, ensuring that the bowl doesn't touch the water. Coat each caramel log with the chocolate, decorate with extra walnuts and return to the tray. Transfer to the refrigerator to set.

Refrigerate in an airtight container for up to 1 week.

Chocolate fruit and nut clusters

Line two baking trays with baking paper.

Place each type of chocolate in separate heatproof bowls over saucepans of simmering water, ensuring the bowls don't touch the water. Stir until the chocolate is melted and smooth. Remove from the heat.

Combine the nuts and dried fruits in a bowl. Stir half into each type of chocolate, mixing thoroughly. Set aside for 10 minutes to allow the chocolate to firm a little. Put small heaped spoonfuls onto the prepared trays. Refrigerate until firm.

The clusters will keep stored in an airtight container, for up to 2 weeks.

NOTE: Sweetened dried cranberries are sometimes sold as craisins.

MAKES 40

125 g (4½ oz) milk chocolate, chopped

125 g (4½ oz) dark chocolate, chopped

80 g (2¾ oz/½ cup) toasted unsalted macadamia nuts, quartered

70 g (2½ oz/½ cup) toasted skinned hazelnuts, halved

75 g (2½ oz/⅓ cup) glacé (candied) ginger pieces, chopped

60 g (2¼ oz/⅓ cup) dried apricots, chopped

40 g (1½ oz/⅓ cup) sweetened dried cranberries (see NOTE)

Portuguese tartlets

MAKES 24

1 tablespoon sugar
2 x 25 cm (10 inch) square sheets ready-rolled puff pastry
plain (all-purpose) flour, for dusting

Custard
3 egg yolks
75 g (2½ oz/⅓ cup) sugar
½ tablespoon custard powder
100 ml (3½ fl oz) milk
80 ml (2½ fl oz/⅓ cup) cream
1 vanilla bean, split lengthways

Preheat the oven to 200°C (400°F/Gas 6). Lightly grease two 12-hole mini muffin tins.

Sprinkle a 30 cm (12 inch) square work surface area with ½ tablespoon sugar. Place one pastry sheet on the sugar, cut in half and sit one half on top of the other. Repeat with the remaining pastry to give a double-layered sheet of pastry. Roll up each sheet of pastry from a short end to form two logs. Wrap each log in plastic wrap and chill in the refrigerator for 10 minutes.

Cut each log into 1 cm (½ inch) rounds. Lightly flour a work surface and roll each disc of pastry into a 10 cm (4 inch) round. Press the pastry rounds into the prepared muffin tins. Prick the bases well with a fork and refrigerate until needed.

To make the custard, place the egg yolks, sugar and custard powder in a saucepan and whisk to combine. Gradually add the milk and cream, whisking until smooth. Add the vanilla bean, place over medium heat and cook, stirring constantly, until the mixture thickens and comes to the boil. Remove the vanilla bean and transfer the custard to a bowl. Cover the surface with plastic wrap (to prevent a skin from forming) and set aside to cool.

Divide the custard among the chilled pastry cases. Do not overfill or the custard will bubble over the pastry. Bake for 12–15 minutes, or until the custard is set and golden. Cool in the tins for 5 minutes before transferring to a wire rack to cool completely.

Mini mud cakes

MAKES 30

170 g (6 oz/¾ cup) caster (superfine) sugar
175 g (6 oz) dark chocolate, chopped
90 g (3¼ oz/⅓ cup) unsalted butter, chopped
60 ml (2 fl oz/¼ cup) water
2 eggs, lightly beaten
2 tablespoons brandy
60 g (2¼ oz/½ cup) plain (all-purpose) flour
60 g (2¼ oz/½ cup) self-raising flour
30 g (1 oz/¼ cup) unsweetened cocoa powder

Chocolate curls
50 g (1¾ oz/⅓ cup) milk chocolate melts
(buttons)

Ganache
200 g (7 oz/1⅓ cups) dark chocolate melts
(buttons), chopped
125 ml (4 fl oz/½ cup) cream

Preheat the oven to 180°C (350°F/Gas 4). Lightly grease the base and sides of a 20 x 30 cm (8 x 12 inch) baking tin. Cover the base and two long sides with baking paper.

Place the sugar, chocolate, butter and water in a small saucepan and stir over low heat for 5 minutes, or until the chocolate melts. Remove from the heat, cool to room temperature then stir in the egg and brandy.

Sift the flours and cocoa into a bowl and make a well in the centre. Pour the chocolate mixture into the well. Mix well and pour into the prepared tin. Bake for 20–25 minutes, or until a skewer inserted in the centre comes out clean. Cool in the tin for 5 minutes before inverting onto a wire rack to cool completely.

Dip a 3 cm (1¼ inch) cookie cutter in hot water and cut out 30 rounds from the cake, re-dipping the cutter between each round (this makes a neater edge). Roll the cut surface gently on the bench to press in any crumbs. Place the mini cakes, top side down, on a wire rack over a baking tray.

To make the chocolate curls, place the chocolate melts in a heatproof bowl. Half-fill a saucepan with water, bring to the boil and remove from the heat. Sit the bowl over the saucepan, ensuring the bowl doesn't touch the water. Stir occasionally until the chocolate has melted. Spread the chocolate fairly thinly over a marble board or a cool baking tray and leave at room temperature until just set. Using the edge of a sharp knife at a 45 degree angle, scrape over the top of the chocolate. The chocolate strips will curl as they come away—don't press too hard. If the chocolate has set too firmly, the curls will break. Leave in a warm place and try again.

To make the ganache, place the chocolate melts in a bowl. Heat the cream in a saucepan until almost boiling, pour over the chocolate and leave for 2 minutes, then stir until the chocolate is melted and smooth. Spoon the chocolate ganache evenly over the cakes, reheating if too thick. Tap the tray gently to settle the chocolate, top each cake with a chocolate curl and allow to set. Use a spatula to remove the cakes from the wire rack. (For image, see page 93.)

Passionfruit ganache tuiles

Place the chocolate in a medium bowl. Strain the passionfruit pulp through a fine sieve and reserve 2 tablespoons pulp. Bring the passionfruit juice to the boil in a small saucepan over medium heat. Simmer for 3–5 minutes, or until reduced by half. Pour over the chocolate and add the reserved passionfruit pulp. Bring the cream to a simmer in a small saucepan. Pour the cream over the chocolate mixture and whisk until smooth. Refrigerate until thick and cold.

Preheat the oven to 180°C (350°F/Gas 4). Line two baking trays with baking paper.

To make the tuile baskets, sift the sugar and flour onto baking paper. Transfer to a medium bowl, add the egg whites and whisk until smooth. Add the butter and whisk until well combined. Place small teaspoons of the mixture onto each baking tray (only cook six biscuits per tray). Use a small spatula to spread each one out to form a 4 cm (1½ inch) disc. Bake one tray at a time for 4–5 minutes, or until the tuiles are light golden. (This allows you to drape the tuiles immediately before they harden.) Remove from the oven and drape tuiles carefully over two wooden spoon handles suspended over a saucepan. Apply pressure to mould each tuile around the spoons. Allow to cool. Repeat with the remaining mixture.

Beat the chilled chocolate mixture until thick and glossy. Spoon or pipe into the cooled tuile baskets and top with the strawberry pieces. Serve immediately.

MAKES 60

250 g (9 oz) white chocolate, roughly chopped
250 ml (9 fl oz/1 cup) passionfruit pulp (about 12 large passionfruit)
80 ml (2½ fl oz/¼ cup) cream
6 large strawberries, hulled and cut into strips

Tuile baskets
60 g (2¼ oz/½ cup) icing (confectioners') sugar
60 g (2¼ oz/½ cup) plain (all-purpose) flour
2 egg whites
60 g (2¼ oz/¼ cup) unsalted butter, melted

97

Rose-scented milk fritters

MAKES 40

100 g (3½ oz/1 cup) powdered milk
50 g (1¾ oz/⅓ cup) blanched almonds, ground
155 g (5½ oz/1¼ cups) plain (all-purpose) flour
1 teaspoon baking powder
½ teaspoon ground cardamom
30 g (1 oz) unsalted butter, chopped
60 g (2¼ oz/¼ cup) plain yoghurt
2–3 tablespoons water
vegetable oil, for deep-frying

Rosewater syrup
220 g (7¾ oz/1 cup) sugar
375 ml (13 fl oz/1½ cups) water
2 drops of rosewater

Sift the dry ingredients into a bowl. Rub in the butter with your fingertips until the mixture resembles fine breadcrumbs. Make a well in the centre and add the yoghurt and water. Mix with a flat-bladed knife to form a soft dough. Shape tablespoons of the mixture into small balls and cover with a damp cloth.

To make the rosewater syrup, combine the sugar and water in a saucepan and stir until the sugar dissolves. Simmer for 5 minutes. Stir in the rosewater.

Fill a heavy-based saucepan one-third full of oil and heat to 180°C (350°F), or until a cube of bread dropped into the oil browns in 15 seconds. Deep-fry the dough balls in batches until deep brown and slightly puffed. Don't cook too quickly or the balls won't cook through. Drain in a sieve set over a bowl. Place the warm balls in a deep bowl and pour the syrup over the top. Leave to soak and cool until still slightly warm. Drain and serve immediately piled in a bowl.

Nutty chocolate fudge

Grease an 18 cm (7 inch) square baking tin and line with baking paper, extending the paper over two opposite sides for easy removal later.

Combine the sugar, evaporated milk and butter in a saucepan over low heat and cook until the sugar dissolves. Increase the heat to medium, bring to the boil and simmer, stirring, for 4–5 minutes. Remove from the heat and stir in the marshmallows and dark chocolate. Continue stirring until smooth, then add the nuts. Pour into the prepared tin and refrigerate until set.

Melt the white chocolate in a heatproof bowl over a saucepan of simmering water, ensuring that the bowl doesn't touch the water.

Remove the chocolate nut mixture from the tin and cut into 1.5 x 4.5 cm (⅝ x 1¾ inch) pieces. Place the pieces on a sheet of baking paper, and use a piping (icing) bag to pipe the white chocolate in drizzly lines over the top. Leave the white chocolate to set before storing or eating.

Store the fudge in an airtight container in the refrigerator. When ready to eat, remove from the refrigerator and leave at room temperature for 10 minutes to allow the fudge to soften slightly.

MAKES 48

370 g (13 oz/2 cups) raw caster (superfine) sugar
170 ml (5½ fl oz/⅔ cup) evaporated milk
20 g (¾ oz) unsalted butter
100 g (3½ oz) white marshmallows
250 g (9 oz/1⅔ cups) chopped dark chocolate
125 g (4½ oz) unsalted mixed nuts, toasted, roughly chopped
60 g (2¼ oz) white chocolate, chopped

Baby strawberry shortcakes

MAKES 36

250 g (9 oz/2 cups) self-raising flour
80 g (2¾ oz/⅓ cup) caster (superfine) sugar
110 g (3¾ oz) unsalted butter, chilled and cut into cubes
1 egg, lightly beaten
125 ml (4 fl oz/½ cup) buttermilk
125 ml (4 fl oz/½ cup) cream
1 tablespoon coffee sugar crystals
¼ teaspoon ground cinnamon
1 teaspoon rosewater
2 tablespoons icing (confectioners') sugar
250 g (9 oz/1⅔ cups) strawberries, hulled and sliced

Preheat the oven to 200°C (400°F/Gas 6). Line two large baking trays with baking paper.

Place the flour and sugar in the bowl of a food processor and pulse briefly. Add 80 g (2¾ oz) of the butter and process until the consistency of fine breadcrumbs. Tip into a large bowl and make a well in the centre.

Whisk the egg, buttermilk and 60 ml (2 fl oz/¼ cup) of the cream in a bowl. Pour onto the flour mixture and mix with a flat-bladed knife until the dough comes together in clumps. Do not overmix.

Drop small teaspoons of the mixture onto the prepared trays. Flatten half with the back of a spoon to make the bases. Melt the remaining butter in a saucepan over low heat. Combine the sugar crystals and cinnamon in a bowl. Brush the tops of the shortcakes with the butter and sprinkle with the cinnamon sugar. Bake for 7–10 minutes, or until risen and golden. Transfer to a wire rack to cool.

Whisk the remaining cream, the rosewater and 1 tablespoon icing sugar until firm peaks form. Spoon the cream onto the bases and top with the strawberry slices and the lids. Dust lightly with the remaining sifted icing sugar. Serve immediately.

The baby shortcakes should be eaten on the same day as baking.

Dressed to the nines

Memorable occasions call for small extravagances —
which is just what you'll find here.

Tangy lemon petits fours

MAKES 36

450 g (1 lb) ready-made Madeira cake
600 g (1 lb 5 oz/4 cups) white chocolate
melts (buttons)
250 ml (9 fl oz/1 cup) cream
6 drops of rose pink food colouring
120 g (4¼ oz) raspberries
icing (confectioners') sugar, sifted, for dusting

Lemon curd
2 large egg yolks
55 g (2 oz/¼ cup) caster (superfine) sugar
½ tablespoon finely grated lemon zest
2½ tablespoons lemon juice
100 g (3½ oz) unsalted butter

To make the lemon curd, beat the egg yolks and sugar in a heatproof bowl. Add the zest, juice and butter and place the bowl over a saucepan of barely simmering water (don't let the bowl touch the water). Stir over low heat for 10 minutes, or until the mixture thickens enough to coat the back of a wooden spoon. Cool slightly, then cover the surface with plastic wrap and leave until completely cold.

Trim the sides of the cake to make a 7.5 x 15 cm (3 x 6 inch) rectangle. Cut the cake horizontally into four slices. Spread two of the slices with the lemon curd and top each with another slice to form two cakes with two layers. Place in the freezer for 20 minutes, or until firm. Cut each cake into 18, 2.5 cm (1 inch) squares. Place on a wire rack with a baking tray underneath.

Place half the white chocolate in a medium bowl. Bring the cream to the boil in a small saucepan over medium heat, pour over the chocolate and stir until smooth. Spoon the melted chocolate over the cakes until covered. Allow to sit for 5 minutes before transferring to a baking tray lined with baking paper. Refrigerate until needed.

Line another baking tray with baking paper. Place the remaining white chocolate in a heatproof bowl over a saucepan of simmering water — do not allow the bowl to touch the water. Add the food colouring and stir until smooth. Spread over the baking paper to a thickness of 1–2 mm (about ¹⁄₁₆ inch) and allow to set. Cut out squares to fit the outside of each petit four. Refrigerate until needed. To serve, top each petit four with a raspberry and dust with the icing sugar.

Tiramisù hearts

Grease and line the base and sides of a 20 x 30 cm (8 x 12 inch) baking tin with baking paper. Line a baking tray with baking paper.

Cut each cake horizontally into three 8 mm (⅜ inch) layers. Combine the coffee, boiling water and liqueur in a small bowl. Set aside to cool. Brush each of the layers with the coffee mixture.

To make the filling, beat the egg, sugar and vanilla in a bowl using electric beaters until pale and creamy. Fold in the mascarpone and cream.

Place one layer of sponge in the prepared tin and spread with one-third of the filling. Top with another layer of sponge. Spread with another one-third of the filling. Repeat with the remaining sponge and filling. Place in the freezer for 40–50 minutes, or until firm. Use a 4 cm (1½ inch) heart-shaped cutter to cut out 24 hearts.

Melt the chocolate in a heatproof bowl over a saucepan of simmering water, ensuring the bowl doesn't touch the water. Stir until the chocolate has melted. Pour onto the prepared tray. Spread to a thickness of 2 mm (¹⁄₁₆ inch) with a spatula. Allow to set before cutting out 24 heart shapes with the cutter used for the cakes.

Transfer the chocolate hearts to a wire rack and dredge half with the cocoa. Place carefully on top of the petits fours. Refrigerate until needed.

MAKES 24

two 14 x 20 cm (5½ x 8 inch) ready-made sponge cakes
1 tablespoon instant coffee powder
60 ml (2 fl oz/¼ cup) boiling water
2 tablespoons coffee liqueur
100 g (3½ oz) dark chocolate, chopped
2 tablespoons unsweetened cocoa powder

Filling
1 large egg
2 tablespoons icing (confectioners') sugar
1 teaspoon natural vanilla extract
150 g (5½ oz) mascarpone cheese
60 ml (2 fl oz/¼ cup) cream, whipped to soft peaks

109

Black forest gâteau petits fours

MAKES 48

455 ml (16 fl oz) cream
2 tablespoons icing (confectioners') sugar
45 ml (1½ fl oz) dark rum
200 g (7 oz/1 cup) morello cherries, drained and finely chopped
100 g (3½ oz) dark chocolate, grated
48 maraschino cherries, with stalks intact

Sponge
125 g (4½ oz/1 cup) plain (all-purpose) flour
2 teaspoons baking powder
60 g (2¼ oz/½ cup) unsweetened cocoa powder
125 g (4½ oz/½ cup) unsalted butter, softened
230 g (8¼ oz/1 cup) caster (superfine) sugar
4 eggs, separated
1 teaspoon natural vanilla extract
170 ml (5½ fl oz/⅔ cup) milk

Preheat the oven to 180°C (350°F/Gas 4). Grease a 20 x 30 cm (8 x 12 inch) baking tin and line with baking paper. Line a baking tray with baking paper.

Sift the flour, baking powder and cocoa. Cream the butter and 145 g (5¼ oz/⅔ cup) sugar until pale and fluffy. Beat in the egg yolks and the vanilla. Fold in the flour mixture and the milk. Beat the egg whites in a clean bowl using electric beaters until light and foamy. Add the remaining sugar to the egg whites and beat until soft peaks form. Stir a tablespoon of the whisked egg white into the sponge mixture, then gently fold in the rest. Pour the mixture into the prepared tin and bake for 25–30 minutes or until firm. Allow to cool for 5 minutes before turning out onto a wire rack.

Beat the cream, sugar and rum in a bowl using electric beaters until firm peaks form. Remove one-third of the cream, cover with plastic wrap and refrigerate. Gently fold the morello cherries through the remaining cream.

Slice the sponge horizontally into three layers. Place the first layer on the prepared baking tray and spread with half the cherries and cream mixture. Top with another layer of sponge, and the remaining cherries and cream mixture. Finish with the remaining slice of sponge and refrigerate for 2 hours, or until firm.

Cut the sponge into 3 cm (1¼ inch) squares. Use a flat-bladed knife to spread one-quarter of the reserved cream around the outside of the petits fours. Coat the outside of the petits fours with the grated chocolate. Spoon cream on top of each petit four and top with a maraschino cherry. Serve chilled.

Raspberry mousse brownies

Preheat the oven to 160°C (315°F/Gas 2–3). Lightly grease a 22 cm (8½ inch) square baking tin and line with baking paper, extending the paper over two opposite sides.

To make the brownie, place the butter and chocolate in a heatproof bowl. Half-fill a saucepan with water and bring to the boil. Sit the bowl over the saucepan, making sure the base of the bowl does not touch the water. Stir occasionally until the butter and chocolate have melted. Cool. Beat the sugar, eggs and vanilla in a bowl with electric beaters until pale and creamy. Fold in the chocolate mixture. Stir in the flour and cocoa. Spread into the prepared tin and bake for 15–20 minutes, or until just cooked. Cool in the tin, then refrigerate for 1 hour before lifting out using the paper handles.

To make the raspberry mousse, place one-quarter of the raspberries and the icing sugar in the bowl of a food processor. Process until smooth. Strain through a fine sieve. Bring the cream and sieved raspberries to the boil in a small saucepan. Add the chocolate melts, remove from the heat and swirl to cover. Allow to sit for 5 minutes. Whisk until smooth. Chill. Refrigerate until needed.

Cut the reserved raspberries in half. Trim the edges of the brownie and cut into rounds, using a 4 cm (1½ inch) cutter. Pipe a little of the mousse onto each round, top with the raspberries and pipe on a little more mousse.

MAKES 25

Brownie
80 g (2¾ oz) unsalted butter, chopped
150 g (5½ oz/1 cup) chopped dark chocolate
115 g (4 oz/½ cup) caster (superfine) sugar
2 small eggs
1 teaspoon natural vanilla extract
60 g (2¼ oz/½ cup) plain (all-purpose) flour, sifted
3 tablespoons cocoa powder, sifted

Raspberry mousse
250 g (9 oz/2 cups) raspberries
1 tablespoon icing (confectioners') sugar
60 ml (2 fl oz/¼ cup) cream
125 g (4½ oz) white chocolate melts (buttons)

Crème caramel petits fours

MAKES 24

200 ml (7 fl oz) milk
145 ml (4¾ fl oz) cream
1 vanilla bean, split lengthways and
seeds scraped
40 g (1½ oz) caster (superfine) sugar
2 large eggs
250 ml (9 fl oz/1 cup) cream, whipped to
soft peaks

Pastry

125 g (4½ oz/½ cup) unsalted butter, chilled and
cut into cubes
155 g (5½ oz/1¼ cups) plain (all-purpose) flour
60 g (2¼ oz/½ cup) icing (confectioners') sugar,
plus extra, sifted, for dusting
1 large egg yolk

Caramel

100 g (3½ oz) caster (superfine) sugar
60 ml (2 fl oz/¼ cup) water

To make the pastry, place the butter and flour in the bowl of a food processor and process until the consistency of fine breadcrumbs. Add the sugar and egg yolk and process until the dough just comes together, adding ½ tablespoon of iced water if necessary. Turn out onto a lightly floured work surface and gather into a ball. Wrap in plastic wrap and refrigerate for 30 minutes.

Preheat the oven to 180°C (350°F/Gas 4). Lightly grease two 12-hole mini muffin tins.

Slice the pastry in half. Roll out each piece between two sheets of baking paper until 2 mm (1⁄16 inch) thick, scattering with flour where necessary. Use a 6 cm (2½ inch) cutter to cut out 24 rounds. Line each prepared tin with a pastry round and trim off any excess. Prick the bases with a fork. Place in the freezer for 5 minutes. Line the bases with baking paper, pour in some baking beads or uncooked rice and bake for 5–7 minutes. Remove the paper and beads and bake for another 3–5 minutes, or until just golden. Allow to cool.

Reduce the oven temperature to 160°C (315°F/Gas 2–3). Grease 24 mini baba tins.

To make the caramel, place the sugar and 45 ml (1½ fl oz) water in a heavy-based saucepan. Bring to the boil, stirring to dissolve the sugar, reduce the heat and simmer, without stirring, for 5–7 minutes, or until golden. Brush any sugar on the side of the pan with a wet pastry brush to avoid crystallising. Do not overcook or the toffee will taste burnt. Very carefully add the remaining water to stop the caramel cooking. (Stand back as the caramel might spit.) Quickly spoon a little of the caramel into the base of each mould before it sets.

Combine the milk, cream and vanilla seeds in a medium saucepan and bring to just below boiling point. Remove from the heat. Whisk the sugar and eggs in a bowl until light and creamy. Pour in the hot milk mixture. Strain through a sieve and remove any excess froth with a spoon. Pour into the prepared baba moulds. Stand the moulds in a large baking tin and pour in hot water to come halfway up the sides of the moulds. Bake for 15 minutes, or until the custard is set. Remove the crème caramels from the water bath and allow to sit for 5 minutes. Then transfer to the refrigerator to chill for 30 minutes. Pipe or spoon a generous swirl of cream into each tart case. Invert the crème caramels over the tart cases, breaking the seal with a sharp thin knife. Spoon over any extra caramel. Serve immediately.

NOTE: The pastry cases and the crème caramel can be prepared ahead of time, but the petits fours should not be assembled until just before serving as the pastry will become soft. (For image, see page 116.)

Raspberry cream sponge petits fours

MAKES 24

two 17 cm (6½ inch) square ready-made
sponge cakes
150 ml (5 fl oz) cream
2 tablespoons icing (confectioners') sugar
250 g (9 oz/2 cups) raspberries

Jelly
80 g (2¾ oz) raspberries
2 tablespoons icing (confectioners') sugar
150 ml (5 fl oz) apple juice
2 teaspoons powdered gelatine
1 tablespoon Cointreau

Spray a 24 cm (9½ inch) square baking tin with oil and line with plastic wrap, extending the plastic wrap over the four sides. Line a baking tray with foil.

To make the jelly, place the raspberries and sugar in the bowl of a food processor and process until smooth. Add 100 ml (3½ fl oz) of the apple juice and strain, discarding the seeds. Bring the remaining apple juice to the boil and sprinkle over the gelatine. Stir until the gelatine dissolves. Add the gelatine mixture and the liqueur to the raspberry juice and stir well. Pour the jelly into the prepared tin. Refrigerate for 2–3 hours, or until set. Transfer to the freezer for 20 minutes.

Slice each cake horizontally into three 5 mm (¼ inch) thick layers. Use a 4 cm (1½ inch) flower cutter to cut out 48 discs. Turn the jelly out onto a work surface. Use the same cutter to cut out 24 flowers.

Whip the cream and sugar to form soft peaks. Spoon into a piping (icing) bag with a large star nozzle. Place 24 cake flowers on the prepared tray. Pipe a small amount of cream on each to secure the jelly. Top with a jelly flower and pipe on a small amount of cream. Place a sponge flower on top, pipe on more cream and decorate with a raspberry. Refrigerate until needed.

These are best eaten on the same day as assembling.

Nougatine and honey butter petits fours

Preheat the oven to 180°C (350°F/Gas 4). Grease a 20 x 30 cm (8 x 12 inch) baking tin and line with baking paper. Line two baking trays with baking paper. Sift the flour, baking powder and ground almonds onto baking paper. Cream the butter and 145 g (5¼ oz/⅔ cup) sugar in a bowl using electric beaters until pale and fluffy. Beat in the egg yolks, then the vanilla. Fold in the flour mixture and milk until just combined. Beat the egg whites in a clean bowl until foamy. Add the remaining sugar and beat into soft peaks. Stir a tablespoonful of the egg white into the sponge mixture, then gently fold in the rest. Pour into the prepared tin and bake for 25–30 minutes or until firm to the touch. Allow to cool in the tin for 5 minutes before turning out onto a rack to cool.

To make the butter cream, beat the butter, honey and vanilla until pale and creamy. Gradually add the sugar and beat until light and fluffy. For the nougatine, combine the sugar, glucose and butter in a frying pan over medium heat. Boil, until the sugar caramelises. Add the almonds and shake the pan to coat. Pour onto the baking tray and cool. Transfer to a food processor and process until finely chopped.

Slice the sponge into three horizontal layers. Place one layer on the remaining prepared tray and spread with one-quarter of the butter cream. Top with another layer of sponge then spread with another quarter of the butter cream. Top with the last layer of sponge then freeze for 30 minutes or until firm. Use a 4 cm 1½ inch) heart cutter to cut out 24 shapes. Spread the sides of half the petits fours with half of the remaining butter cream. Spread the tops of the remaining petits fours with the remaining butter cream. Coat the sides and tops with nougatine. Serve chilled.

MAKES 24

Sponge
125 g (4½ oz/1 cup) plain (all-purpose) flour
2 teaspoons baking powder
55 g (2 oz/½ cup) ground almonds
125 g (4½ oz/½ cup) unsalted butter, softened
230 g (8¼ oz/1 cup) caster (superfine) sugar
4 eggs, separated
1 teaspoon natural vanilla extract
170 ml (5½ fl oz/⅔ cup) milk

Honey butter cream
100 g (3½ oz) unsalted butter, softened
40 g (1½ oz) honey
1 teaspoon natural vanilla extract
200 g (7 oz) icing (confectioners') sugar, sifted

Nougatine
65 g (2½ oz) sugar
65 ml (2¼ fl oz) liquid glucose
65 g (2½ oz) unsalted butter
65 g (2½ oz) chopped blanched almonds

Mini pavlovas

MAKES 40

3 egg whites
125 g (4½ oz/1 cup) icing (confectioners') sugar
150 g (5½ oz) dark chocolate, melted
250 ml (9 fl oz/1 cup) thick (double/heavy) cream
1 tablespoon icing (confectioners') sugar, extra, sifted
1 teaspoon finely grated orange zest
assorted fresh fruit (such as strawberries, papaya and kiwi fruit), sliced, to serve
passionfruit pulp, to serve

Preheat the oven to 150°C (300°F/Gas 2). Line two baking trays with baking paper and use a 4 cm (1½ inch) cutter as a guide to draw 20 circles on each sheet of paper. Invert the paper on the trays (so the pencil won't come off on the pavlovas).

Place the egg whites in a large heatproof bowl and beat with electric beaters until stiff peaks form. Set the bowl over a saucepan of simmering water, carefully add the sugar and beat until the mixture is thick and glossy.

Spread a little of the meringue mixture, following the marked rounds as a guide, over each sheet of baking paper—these will be the bases of the pavlovas. Spoon the remaining meringue mixture into a piping bag fitted with a 5 mm (¼ inch) plain piping (icing) nozzle. Pipe three small circles one on top of the other around the outer edge of each base to form a border. Bake for 30 minutes, or until firm to the touch. Cool in the oven with the door slightly ajar.

When completely cool, dip the base of each pavlova in the melted chocolate to come about 2 mm (¹⁄₁₆ inch) up the side, then transfer to trays lined with baking paper and leave to set.

Place the cream, extra icing sugar and orange zest in a bowl and stir to combine. If necessary, lightly beat until just thick. Spoon into a piping bag fitted with a small plain nozzle and pipe onto the pavlovas. Top with the fruit and serve with the passionfruit pulp.

Orange cheesecake petits fours

Lightly grease a 20 x 30 cm (8 x 12 inch) baking tin and line with baking paper.

To make the cheesecake, beat the cream cheese, vanilla and sugar in a medium bowl using electric beaters until smooth. Add the eggs yolks and beat well. Stir in the melted chocolate, orange zest, juice and Cointreau. Pour the water into a small bowl, sprinkle over the gelatine and stir until completely dissolved. Stir into the cheesecake mixture. Beat the egg whites in a clean bowl with electric beaters to form soft peaks. Fold into the cheesecake mixture along with the cream. Trim the edges of the cake. Slice horizontally into 5 mm (¼ inch) thick slices. Line the base of the prepared tin with a single layer of the cake, cutting where necessary to fit. Pour over the cheesecake mixture. Form another layer with the remaining cake and press down firmly. Fold over the baking paper and wrap firmly in foil. Refrigerate for 2 hours.

To make the ganache, bring the cream to the boil in a saucepan. Place the chocolate in a heatproof bowl. Add the cream. Stand for 5 minutes, then stir until smooth.

Use a 4 cm (1½ inch) cutter dipped in hot water to cut the cheesecake into 36 rounds. Place on a wire rack. Spoon the ganache over the tops until coated.

To make the caramelised orange zest, place the sugar in a frying pan over medium heat and cook until the sugar begins to caramelise. Add the zest and shake the pan to coat. Cool. Arrange on the tops. Refrigerate until needed.

MAKES 36

Cheesecake
200 g (7 oz) white chocolate, melted
250 g (9 oz/1 cup) cream cheese,
   at room temperature
1 teaspoon natural vanilla extract
80 g (2¾ oz/⅓ cup) caster (superfine) sugar
2 eggs, separated
2 teaspoons finely grated orange zest
3 tablespoons strained orange juice
2 tablespoons Cointreau
60 ml (2 fl oz/¼ cup) boiling water
15 g (½ oz) powdered gelatine
150 ml (5 fl oz) cream, whipped to firm peaks
450 g (1 lb) ready-made Madeira cake

White chocolate ganache
250 ml (9 fl oz/1 cup) cream
600 g (1 lb 5 oz/4 cups) white chocolate
   melts (buttons)

Caramelised orange zest
zest of 2 oranges, cut into 3cm (1¼ inch) strips
55 g (2 oz/¼ cup) caster (superfine) sugar

Baileys and white chocolate opera

Line two baking trays with baking paper. To make the Baileys butter cream, place the chocolate in a heatproof bowl. Half-fill a saucepan with water and bring to the boil. Sit the bowl over the saucepan, making sure the base of the bowl does not touch the water. Stir occasionally until melted. Cream the butter and sugar in a small bowl until light and fluffy. Add the Baileys and chocolate and beat until smooth.

Trim the sponges to 3 cm (1¼ inches) in thickness. Slice each sponge into three horizontal layers. Place the first layer on one side of a prepared tray and spread with one-quarter of the butter cream. Repeat with the second layer and another quarter of the butter cream. Top with the last layer of cake. Repeat on the other side of the tray with the other cake and butter cream, reserving enough cream for the tops, and place both cakes in the freezer for 20 minutes, or until firm. Cut each cake into 12 squares.

Lightly beat the egg white in a small bowl. Pierce a blueberry with a skewer, dip into the egg white and sprinkle with the sugar. Transfer to a plate. Repeat with the remaining blueberries and set aside.

Pour the melted chocolate onto the remaining prepared tray. Spread to a thickness of 2 mm (¹⁄₁₆ inch). Allow to set before cutting into 24 squares the same size as the petits fours. Spread a small amount of the butter cream on top of each petit four and top with the chocolate. Place butter cream in the centre of each and top with a blueberry.

MAKES 24

two 14 x 20 cm (5½ x 8 inch) ready-made
   sponge cakes
1 egg white
24 blueberries
115 g (4 oz/½ cup) caster (superfine) sugar
100 g (3½ oz) white chocolate, melted

Baileys butter cream
250 g (9 oz) white chocolate, chopped
185 g (6½ oz/¾ cup) unsalted butter, softened
30 g (1 oz/¼ cup) icing (confectioners') sugar
2½ tablespoons Baileys Irish Cream

Caramel walnut mini gâteaux

MAKES 48

Sponge

250 g (9 oz/2½ cups) walnut halves, lightly toasted
100 g (3½ oz) unsalted butter, softened
150 g (5½ oz) caster (superfine) sugar
3 egg yolks
100 g (3½ oz) self-raising flour, sifted
5 egg whites

Filling

250 ml (9 fl oz/1 cup) milk
55 g (2 oz/¼ cup) caster (superfine) sugar
2 egg yolks
1 teaspoon natural vanilla extract
2 tablespoons cornflour (cornstarch)
250 ml (9 fl oz/1 cup) cream, whipped to soft peaks

Caramelised walnuts

55 g (2 oz/¼ cup) caster (superfine) sugar
85 g (3 oz) walnut halves

Preheat the oven to 180°C (350°F/Gas 4). Grease a 20 x 30 cm (8 x 12 inch) baking tin and line the base and sides with baking paper.

To make the sponge, place the walnuts in the bowl of a food processor and pulse in short bursts until coarsely chopped. Cream the butter and sugar in a large bowl with electric beaters until pale and fluffy. Use a metal spoon to fold in the egg yolks, 100 g (3½ oz) of the walnuts and the flour. Whisk the egg whites in a separate large bowl using electric beaters until medium peaks form. Stir 1 tablespoonful of the whisked whites into the sponge mixture, then gently fold in the rest using a large metal spoon. Pour the mixture into the prepared tin and bake for 20–25 minutes, or until firm to the touch. Allow to cool in the tin for 5 minutes before turning out onto a wire rack to cool completely.

To make the filling, bring 185 ml (6 fl oz/¾ cup) of the milk and half the sugar to a simmer in a medium saucepan over medium heat. Beat the remaining milk and sugar, the egg yolks, vanilla and cornflour in a separate bowl. Gradually pour in the hot milk mixture, whisking constantly. Return the mixture to the cleaned saucepan and cook over medium–high heat, whisking constantly until thick. Allow to cool for 10 minutes. Transfer to a bowl and press a piece of plastic wrap onto the top of the filling to seal. Refrigerate until chilled. Beat the filling with the electric beaters until smooth. Gently fold in the whipped cream.

Cut the sponge in half horizontally. Place the first layer onto a baking tray lined with baking paper. Spread evenly with 250 ml (9 fl oz/1 cup) of the filling. Place the remaining layer on top. Transfer to the freezer and chill for 30 minutes, or until firm.

To make the caramelised walnuts, place the sugar in a small frying pan over medium heat and cook until beginning to caramelise. Add the walnuts and shake the pan to coat. Set aside to cool.

Trim the edges of the sponge. Slice into 3 cm (1¼ inch) squares using a very sharp serrated knife. Spread the sides of the petits fours with the filling, using a flat-bladed knife. Coat the sides evenly with the remaining chopped walnuts. Use a piping (icing) bag to pipe swirls with the remaining filling on the top of the petits fours. Garnish each with a caramelised walnut. Refrigerate until needed. (For image, see page 132.)

Rum and raisin petits fours

60 ml (2 fl oz/¼ cup) cream, whipped to soft peaks
icing (confectioners') sugar, sifted, for dusting
24 edible sugar stars or similar

Chocolate sponge
125 g (4½ oz/1 cup) plain (all-purpose) flour
2 teaspoons baking powder
60 g (2¼ oz/½ cup) unsweetened cocoa powder
125 g (4½ oz/½ cup) unsalted butter, softened
230 g (8¼ oz/1 cup) caster (superfine) sugar
4 eggs, separated
1 teaspoon natural vanilla extract
170 ml (5½ fl oz/⅔ cup) milk

Filling
200 g (7 oz) dark chocolate, chopped
30 g (1 oz/¼ cup) raisins, finely chopped
3 tablespoons dark rum
60 ml (2 fl oz/¼ cup) milk
2 teaspoons powdered gelatine
200 ml (7 fl oz) cream, whipped to soft peaks

Ganache
125 ml (4 fl oz/½ cup) cream
200 g (7 oz) dark chocolate, chopped

Chocolate circles
100 g (3½ oz/⅔ cup) chocolate melts (buttons)

Preheat the oven to 180°C (350°F/Gas 4). Grease a 20 x 30 cm (8 x 12 inch) baking tin and line the base and sides with baking paper.

To make the chocolate sponge, sift the flour, baking powder and cocoa onto baking paper. Cream the butter and 145 g (5¼ oz/⅔ cup) of the sugar until pale and fluffy. Beat in the egg yolks, one at a time, and the vanilla. Fold in the flour mixture and the milk until just combined. Beat the egg whites in a clean bowl until light and foamy. Sprinkle the remaining sugar into the egg whites and beat until soft peaks form. Stir a tablespoonful of the whisked egg whites into the sponge mixture, then gently fold in the rest using a large metal spoon. Pour the mixture into the prepared tin and bake for 25–30 minutes, or until firm to the touch. Allow to cool in the tin for 5 minutes before turning out onto a wire rack to cool completely.

To make the filling, place the chocolate in a heatproof bowl. Half-fill a saucepan with water and bring to the boil. Sit the bowl over the saucepan, making sure the base of the bowl does not touch the water. Stir occasionally until smooth. Combine the raisins and rum in a small bowl. Bring the milk to the boil, sprinkle over the gelatine and whisk until combined (it may look curdled). Add to the melted chocolate along with the raisin mixture. Whisk until smooth. Set aside to cool. Fold the cream into the cooled chocolate mixture.

Slice the sponge in half horizontally. Place one layer on a baking tray lined with baking paper and spread with the filling. Top with the remaining layer of sponge. Place in the refrigerator for 2 hours, or until it is firm.

To make the ganache, bring the cream to the boil in a small saucepan. Place the chocolate in a heatproof bowl and add the cream. Allow to sit for 5 minutes. Whisk until smooth.

Use a 4 cm (1½ inch) cutter to cut out 24 rounds from the sponge. Place the rounds on a wire rack over a baking tray. Spoon the ganache over the petits fours until completely covered. You may need to reheat the ganache gently as you go. Refrigerate until needed.

Meanwhile, to make the chocolate circles, melt the chocolate and pour onto a baking tray greased and covered with baking paper. Spread to a thickness of 2 mm (⅟₁₆ inch) with a spatula and allow to set. Cut out 24 rounds with the same cutter used for the petits fours.

Secure a chocolate circle to the top of each petit four with a dob of cream. Dust with the icing sugar and attach the sugar shapes with another dob of cream. Refrigerate until needed. (For image, see page 133.)

Cranberry and fig mini puddings

MAKES 24

four 3 cm (1¼ inch) thick slices white bread
5 egg yolks
100 g (3½ oz) caster (superfine) sugar
2 teaspoons finely grated orange zest
600 ml (21 fl oz) cream
1 vanilla bean, split lengthways and
seeds scraped
60 g (2¼ oz/½ cup) sweetened dried cranberries
(see NOTE page 91)
100 g (3½ oz) dried apricots, roughly chopped
100 g (3½ oz) dried figs, roughly chopped
icing (confectioners') sugar, sifted, for
dusting (optional)

Preheat the oven to 150°C (300°F/Gas 2). Grease and line a 20 x 30 cm (8 x 12 inch) baking tin with baking paper, extending the paper over the four sides for easy removal later.

Remove the crusts from the bread and cut into 3 cm (1¼ inch) cubes.

Beat the egg yolks and sugar in a small bowl with electric beaters until light and creamy. Add the zest and beat again briefly. Pour the cream into a saucepan and add the vanilla seeds. Bring to the boil and pour over the egg mixture, whisking constantly. Add the bread and toss to coat. Sprinkle half of the fruit into the prepared tin. Top with a layer of bread. Scatter with the remaining fruit and pour over the remaining egg mixture. Bake for 45–50 minutes, or until firm when tested with a skewer. Allow to cool completely in the tin. Transfer to the refrigerator and chill for at least 4 hours, or until firm.

Invert the pudding onto a cutting board or work surface and remove the paper. Use a 4 cm (1½ inch) cutter to cut out 24 rounds (or cut with a sharp serrated knife). (Cutting from the base is easier due to the bread becoming crisp on the top.) Dust with the icing sugar, if desired, and serve chilled.

Strawberry princess petits fours

MAKES 48

two 17 cm (6½ inch) round ready-made
sponge cakes
3 x 250 g (9 oz) packets ready-to-roll marzipan
48 edible sugar flowers

Strawberry cream
250 g (9 oz/1⅔ cups) strawberries, hulled
200 g (7 oz) white chocolate, chopped
250 g (9 oz) mascarpone cheese
30 g (1 oz/¼ cup) icing (confectioners')
sugar, sifted
60 ml (2 fl oz/¼ cup) strawberry liqueur
2 teaspoons powdered gelatine
2½ tablespoons boiling water

White chocolate ganache
375 ml (13 fl oz/1½ cups) cream
600 g (1 lb 5 oz/4 cups) white chocolate
melts (buttons)
10–14 drops of red food colouring (depending
on shade desired)

To make the strawberry cream, place the strawberries in the bowl of a food processor and process until smooth. Strain through a fine sieve. Discard the pulp. Place the chocolate in a heatproof bowl. Half-fill a saucepan with water and bring to the boil. Sit the bowl over the saucepan, making sure the base of the bowl does not touch the water. Stir occasionally until melted. Beat the mascarpone, strawberry puree, sugar and liqueur in a medium bowl with electric beaters until light and creamy. Sprinkle the gelatine over the water and stir until dissolved. Set aside to cool. Add the cooled gelatine mixture and the melted chocolate to the mascarpone mixture and beat until smooth.

Grease and line the base and sides of a 20 x 30 cm (8 x 12 inch) baking tin with baking paper, extending the paper over the long sides for easy removal later.

Trim the sides of each sponge to form a square. Cut the sponges horizontally into 5 mm (¼ inch) thick slices. Arrange one-third of the sponge slices in a thin layer on the base of the prepared tin, trimming where necessary. Pour over half the strawberry cream and spread to an even thickness. Add another one-third of the sponge slices and spread the remaining strawberry cream on top. Finish with a layer of the remaining sponge slices. Wrap firmly in foil and refrigerate for 4 hours, or until firm.

To make the white chocolate ganache, bring the cream to the boil in a small saucepan. Place the chocolate in a heatproof bowl and add the cream. Allow to sit for 5 minutes. Add the food colouring and whisk until smooth.

Place the sponge cake on a cutting board and cut into rounds using a 3 cm (1¼ inch) cutter. Roll out one packet of marzipan to a thickness of 2 mm (⅟₁₆ inch) between two sheets of baking paper, sprinkling with icing sugar where necessary. Cut out 16 round tops with the same cutter used for the petits fours. Cut out 16 10 x 3 cm (4 x 1¼ inch) strips for the sides. Repeat with the remaining marzipan. Attach a marzipan strip to the side of a petits four. Seal the join with a small flat-bladed knife. Place a marzipan round on top and seal with the knife. Repeat with the remaining

marzipan and petits fours. (You may need to use a little of the ganache to attach the marzipan.) Use a wet flat-bladed knife to smooth the surface.

Place the petits fours on a wire rack over a baking tray. Spoon the ganache over the top until completely covered. You may need to gently reheat the ganache as you go. Refrigerate for 2 hours, or until firm. Decorate with the sugar flowers and serve. (For image, see page 140.)

Chocolate mousse and cherry liqueur cups

Place the chocolate in a heatproof bowl over a saucepan of simmering water, ensuring the bowl doesn't touch the water. Stir until the chocolate has melted. Paint the inside of 12 small paper cups evenly with half the chocolate. Place on a baking tray and transfer to the freezer until set. Paint on another layer of chocolate until evenly coated. Freeze again until firm. Carefully peel off the paper cases.

Combine the cherries and brandy or liqueur in a small bowl. Cover and refrigerate until needed.

To make the chocolate mousse, place the melted chocolate, cream and egg in a medium bowl and beat until smooth. Refrigerate for 1 hour, or until firm.

Pipe or spoon the mousse into the chocolate cups. Top each cup with a white chocolate melt and finish with a cherry.

MAKES 12

150 g (5½ oz/1 cup) dark chocolate, chopped
12 tinned pitted black cherries in
  syrup, drained
1 tablespoon brandy or cherry liqueur
150 g (5½ oz/1 cup) white chocolate
  melts (buttons)

Chocolate mousse
160 g (5¾ oz) dark chocolate, melted
80 ml (2½ fl oz/⅓ cup) cream
1 small egg

Tropical passion petits fours

MAKES 48

450 g (1 lb) ready-made Madeira cake or
sponge cake
80 g (2¾ oz/¼ cup) raspberry jam
125 ml (4 fl oz/½ cup) cream,
whipped to stiff peaks
60 g (2¼ oz/1 cup) shredded coconut,
lightly toasted

Passionfruit filling
250 g (9 oz/1 cup) cream cheese, at
room temperature
150 g (5½ oz) mascarpone cheese
60 g (2¼ oz/½ cup) icing (confectioners') sugar
2 teaspoons powdered gelatine
1½ tablespoons boiling water
125 ml (4 fl oz/½ cup) passionfruit pulp (about
4 large passionfruit)

White chocolate ganache
250 ml (9 fl oz/1 cup) cream
400 g (14 oz) white chocolate, chopped

Grease a 20 x 30 cm (8 x 12 inch) baking tin and line with baking paper, extending the paper over long sides for easy removal later.

To make the passionfruit filling, beat the cream cheese, mascarpone and sugar in a medium bowl until smooth. Sprinkle the gelatine over the water and stir until dissolved. Add the gelatine mixture and passionfruit to the cream cheese mixture and beat until smooth.

Cut the cake vertically into 5 mm (¼ inch) thick slices. Heat the jam in a small saucepan. Arrange one-third of the cake slices in a thin layer on the base of the prepared tin, trimming where necessary. Spread on half the jam. Pour on half the passionfruit filling and spread to an even thickness. Repeat with another layer of cake slices and the remaining jam and filling. Finish with a layer of the remaining cake slices. Wrap firmly in foil and refrigerate for 4 hours, or until firm.

To make the ganache, bring the cream to the boil in a small saucepan. Place the chocolate in a heatproof bowl and add the cream. Allow to sit for 5 minutes. Whisk until smooth.

Place the cake on a cutting board and using a very sharp knife dipped in boiling water cut into 2.5 cm (1 inch) squares. Place on a wire rack over a baking tray and spoon the ganache over the petits fours until completely covered. Coat the sides with the coconut and refrigerate until needed.

Mini hazelnut and chocolate dacquoise

To make the chocolate mousse, place the chocolate in a heatproof bowl. Half-fill a saucepan with water and bring to the boil. Sit the bowl over the saucepan, making sure the bowl does not touch the water. Stir occasionally until smooth. Bring the milk to the boil, sprinkle on the gelatine and whisk until combined. Pour into the melted chocolate, add the liqueur and stir until smooth. Set aside to cool. Fold in the cream and refrigerate until needed.

Preheat the oven to 180°C (350°F/Gas 4). Grease and line the base and sides of two 24 x 30 cm (9½ x 12 inch) baking tins.

To make the dacquoise, combine the ground hazelnuts and caster sugar in a bowl. Beat the egg whites in a large bowl until soft peaks form. Slowly add the icing sugar, beating well until the mixture is firm and glossy. Gently fold in the hazelnut mixture. Spoon the mixture evenly into the prepared tins and spread out to an even thickness. Bake for 15–20 minutes, or until golden and firm to the touch. Cut out 24 rounds using a 4 cm (1½ inch) cutter while still warm.

To assemble, spoon the mousse into a piping (icing) bag with a large star nozzle and pipe onto 8 dacquoise rounds. Top each with another dacquoise round and pipe on a layer of mousse. Place a dacquoise round on top and dust with icing sugar. Place in the freezer until ready to serve.

These are beautiful straight from the freezer on a hot day. They can also be served chilled.

MAKES 8

Chocolate mousse
150 g (5½ oz/1 cup) chopped dark chocolate
60 ml (2 fl oz/¼ cup) milk
2 teaspoons powdered gelatine
2 tablespoons coffee liqueur
200 ml (7 fl oz) cream, whipped to soft peaks

Dacquoise
85 g (3 oz) ground hazelnuts
80 g (2¾ oz/⅓ cup) caster (superfine) sugar
6 egg whites
75 g (2½ oz) icing (confectioners') sugar, plus extra, sifted, for dusting

Almond and hazelnut triangles

MAKES 48

200 g (7 oz) flaked almonds, lightly toasted
250 g (9 oz/1⅔ cups) strawberries, hulled
and quartered

Sponge
125 g (4½ oz/1 cup) plain (all-purpose) flour
2 teaspoons baking powder
55 g (2 oz/½ cup) ground hazelnuts
125 g (4½ oz/½ cup) unsalted butter, softened
230 g (8¼ oz/1 cup) caster (superfine) sugar
4 eggs, separated
1 teaspoon natural vanilla extract
1 teaspoon finely grated orange zest
170 ml (5½ fl oz/⅔ cup) milk

Hazelnut meringue frosting
3 large egg whites
230 g (8¼ oz/1 cup) caster (superfine) sugar
250 g (9 oz/1 cup) unsalted butter,
cut into cubes
2 tablespoons Frangelico

Preheat the oven to 180°C (350°F/Gas 4). Grease a 20 x 30 cm (8 x 12 inch) baking tin and line with baking paper, extending the paper over the long sides for easy removal later. Line a baking tray with baking paper.

To make the sponge, sift the flour, baking powder and ground hazelnuts onto baking paper. Cream the butter and 145 g (5¼ oz/⅔ cup) of the sugar until pale and fluffy. Beat in the egg yolks, one at a time, beating well after each addition. Beat in the vanilla and orange zest. Fold in the flour mixture and the milk until just combined. Beat the egg whites in a clean bowl until light and foamy. Sprinkle the remaining sugar onto the egg whites and beat until soft peaks form. Stir a tablespoonful of the whisked egg white into the sponge mixture, then gently fold in the rest using a large metal spoon. Pour the mixture into the prepared tin and bake for 20–25 minutes, or until firm to the touch. Allow to cool in the tin for 5 minutes before turning out onto a wire rack to cool completely.

To make the hazelnut meringue frosting, place the egg whites and sugar in a heatproof bowl over a saucepan of simmering water, do not let the bowl touch the water. Stir to dissolve the sugar, taking care not to cook the egg whites. When the sugar has dissolved, remove from the heat and beat with electric beaters for 5 minutes, or until soft peaks form. Add the butter, cube by cube, beating well after each addition. Add the liqueur and beat well.

Cut the sponge horizontally into three layers. Place the first layer on the prepared tray and spread with one-third of the frosting. Top with another layer of sponge and another third of the frosting. Add the remaining layer of sponge. Refrigerate for 2 hours, or until firm.

Cut the sponge into 24, 5 x 4 cm (2 x 1½ inch) rectangles. Slice each rectangle on the diagonal to make triangles. Spread half the remaining frosting evenly over the sides of the petits fours with a spatula. Coat the sides in the almonds. Fill a piping (icing) bag with the remaining frosting and pipe on top of the petits fours. Garnish with a piece of strawberry and serve chilled. (For image, see page 150.)

Christening petit fours

MAKES 48

two 14 x 20 cm (5½ x 8 inch) ready-made
sponge cakes
160 g (5¾ oz/½ cup) apricot jam
1 tablespoon rum (optional)
3 x 500 g (1 lb 2 oz) packets ready-made
white icing
icing (confectioners') sugar, sifted, for dusting
blue or pink food colouring
48 edible sugar decorations
1 egg white, lightly beaten

Filling
250 ml (9 fl oz/1 cup) milk
55 g (2 oz/¼ cup) caster (superfine) sugar
2 egg yolks
1 teaspoon natural vanilla extract
2 tablespoons cornflour (cornstarch)
2 teaspoons powdered gelatine
60 ml (2 fl oz/¼ cup) boiling water
250 ml (9 fl oz/1 cup) cream,
whipped to firm peaks

Sugar syrup
200 g (7 oz) sugar
100 ml (3½ fl oz) water

To make the filling, bring 185 ml (6 fl oz/¾ cup) of the milk and half the sugar to a simmer in a medium saucepan over medium heat. Whisk the remaining milk and sugar, the egg yolks, vanilla and cornflour in a bowl. Gradually pour in the hot milk, whisking constantly. Return the mixture to the clean saucepan and cook over medium–high heat, whisking constantly, until thick. Allow to cool for 10 minutes. Transfer to a bowl. Press a piece of plastic wrap onto the top of the filling to seal. Refrigerate until just chilled. Sprinkle the gelatine over the water and stir until dissolved. Set aside to cool. Beat the gelatine into the filling mixture using electric beaters. Fold the cream into the mixture until well combined.

Grease and line the base of a 20 x 30 cm (8 x 12 inch) baking tin with baking paper, extending over the long sides for easy removal later.

Cut each sponge cake horizontally into two even slices. Place two slices of the sponge in the prepared tin, to form one layer. Warm the jam and rum in a small saucepan and spread evenly over the sponge.

Pour the filling over the top and spread to an even thickness. Finish with a layer of the remaining sponge slices. Transfer to the refrigerator for 2–3 hours (or the freezer for 1 hour) and chill until firm. Trim the outside and cut into 48, 2.5 cm (1 inch) squares.

Place in the refrigerator until needed.

To make the sugar syrup, bring the sugar and water to the boil in a small saucepan. Allow to cool.

Slice each packet of icing in half and wrap each half in plastic wrap to avoid it drying out. Place a sheet of baking paper on a work surface and sprinkle with the icing sugar. Knead 3–4 drops of colouring into a piece of icing. Roll out to a 30 cm (12 inch) square sprinkling with icing sugar as needed. Cut into 7 cm (2¾ inch) squares. Brush the outside of a sponge square with sugar syrup to attach the icing. Carefully remove a square of icing and place over the top of the sponge square. Gently press over the cake with the tips of your fingers dusted with icing sugar. Smooth and trim the excess. Repeat with the remaining icing, sugar syrup and sponge squares. Brush the backs of the sugar decorations with egg white and attach to the top of the petits fours. Refrigerate until needed.
(For image, see page 151.)

Rosewater meringues with raspberry cream

Preheat the oven to 120°C (235°F/Gas ½). Line two baking trays with baking paper and mark 30, 3 cm (1¼ inch) rounds on each sheet of paper.

Beat the egg whites in a large bowl with electric beaters until stiff peaks form. Add the sugar gradually, beating well after each addition, and continue to beat until thick and glossy. Add the rosewater and food colouring, if using, to tint the meringue pale pink. Transfer the mixture, in batches if necessary, to a piping (icing) bag fitted with a 1 cm (½ inch) plain nozzle. Following the marked rounds as a guide, pipe 60 rounds, about 2 cm (¾ inch) high, onto the paper. Bake for 1 hour. Leave to cool in the oven with the door slightly ajar.

To make the sugared rose petals, if using, remove the petals from the roses. Use a small paintbrush to lightly brush the egg white over both sides of each petal. Toss lightly in the sugar and set aside to dry. Repeat with the remaining petals.

To make the raspberry cream, beat the cream and sugar until thick, fold in the raspberries. Spread the raspberry cream over the base of half the meringues and sandwich with the remaining meringues. Decorate with the sugared rose petals, if using.

Unfilled meringues will keep, stored in an airtight container in a cool place, for up to 2 weeks.

MAKES 30

4 egg whites
230 g (8¼ oz/1 cup) caster (superfine) sugar
1 tablespoon rosewater
few drops of pink food colouring (optional)

Sugared rose petals (optional)
2–3 unsprayed pink or red roses
1 egg white, lightly beaten
115 g (4 oz/½ cup) caster (superfine) sugar

Raspberry cream
300 ml (10½ fl oz) thick (double/heavy) cream
1 tablespoon icing (confectioners') sugar, sifted
100 g (3½ oz) fresh raspberries or thawed
  frozen raspberries

Index

Published in 2009 by Murdoch Books Pty Limited

Murdoch Books Australia
Pier 8/9
23 Hickson Road
Millers Point NSW 2000
Phone: +61 (0) 2 8220 2000
Fax: +61 (0) 2 8220 2558
www.murdochbooks.com.au

Murdoch Books UK Limited
Erico House, 6th Floor
93–99 Upper Richmond Road
Putney, London SW15 2TG
Phone: +44 (0) 20 8785 5995
Fax: +44 (0) 20 8785 5985
www.murdochbooks.co.uk

Publisher: Jane Lawson
Project manager: Jane Massam
Editor: Megan Johnston
Food editor: Chrissy Freer
Design Concept: Reuben Crossman
Design layout: Helen Beard
Photographer: Brett Stevens
Stylist: Matt Page
Food preparation: Grace Campbell and Kim Meredith
Recipes by: Kim Meredith and the Murdoch Books
test kitchen
Production: Kita George

National Library of Australia Cataloguing-in-Publication Data
Title: Indulgence Petits Fours: a fine selection of sweet treats
ISBN: 9781741961188 (hbk)
Series: Indulgence series
Notes: Includes index
Subjects: Cake
Dewey Number: 641.865

A catalogue record for this book is available from the
British Library.

Colour separation by SPLITTING IMAGE.

PRINTED IN CHINA.

The Publisher and stylist would like to thank Cotton Love,
Design Mode International, Ici Et La, Le Bon Bon, Macleay on
Manning, One Small Room, Pigott's store, Top 3 by Design,
Waterford Wedgwood for lending equipment for use and
photography.

IMPORTANT: Those who might be at risk from the effects of
salmonella poisoning (the elderly, pregnant women, young
children and those suffering from immune deficiency
diseases) should consult their doctor with any concerns about
eating raw eggs.

OVEN GUIDE: You may find cooking times vary depending
on the oven you are using. For fan-forced ovens, as a general
rule, set the oven temperature to 20°C (35°F) lower than
indicated in the recipe.